EXPOSITION

OF

TWENTY-EIGHT PARABLES

TO

MY WIFE

An Exposition of Twenty-Eight Parables of Our Lord

BY

The Rev. GEORGE CHRISTIE, D.D.,
ST ANDREW'S, EDINBURGH.

Church of Scotland
COMMITTEE ON PUBLICATIONS
121 GEORGE STREET, EDINBURGH, AND
232 ST VINCENT STREET, GLASGOW

1934

FOREWORD.

THIS book is of the type of the Guild text-books which were issued during the last generation by the Committee on Christian Life and Work, and which in recent years have been under the editorial charge of Dr Christie. In the series one of the most valued is Dr James Robertson's exposition of " Our Lord's Teaching," which has had a circulation approaching 75,000 copies, and the following study of the Parables of our Lord will be found a useful supplement to that popular manual. It should be welcomed by teachers of Bible Classes when working through a syllabus that covers the central and vital subject. It will also be found suggestive and helpful by the expository preacher, as it sums up the message of some of the Parables in felicitous phrases, while, at the writer's best, the detailed analysis and the skilful divisions remind us of the treatment of the Parable of the Sower in one of the great expository sermons of Robertson of Brighton. What Dr Christie has given us is so good that the reader will regret the self-imposed limitation in the matter of plan and scale, and it may be expected that the modest volume will have a reception that will lead him to give it to the Church in an extended form.

W. P. PATERSON.

UNIVERSITY OF EDINBURGH,
    10th March 1934.

CONTENTS.

7

CONTENTS

I.

THE
COMING OF THE KINGDOM:
SOWING AND GROWING.

THE SOWER AND THE SOIL

or,

HOW MEN RECEIVE THE GOSPEL.

S. MATTHEW, xiii. 1-23.   S. MARK, iv. 1-20.   S. LUKE, viii. 4-15.

THIS is initially a piece of autobiography, giving the results of our Lord's experience and His expectation for the future in the matter of preaching and hearing ; it is a Record and a Prophecy.   He is speaking to men about themselves, holding up a mirror, showing how and why they succeed or fail in receiving messages of truth.

I. SOWING.

(1) THE SEED is the Word of God, the Word of the Kingdom.   God's Word is faultless, always good, always with a seed's possibility of growth and harvest. If harvest does not come the blame does not attach to the Seed.

The Seed is a gift to the Soil, coming from above ; the Word of God is offered to man by the grace of God.   The Harvest is the Soil's Return to the Sower.

The Problem of the Parable is of supreme importance : the coming together of Seed and Soil, the Word of God and the Heart of Man.   For Harvest the Soil requires the Seed ; for Growth the Seed requires the Soil : each is necessary to the other.

(2) THE SOWER is originally the Master Himself ; now all sincere preachers, teachers, missionaries and messengers of His Evangel. In giving His experience and expectation He prepares His followers of every age for failures, as well as encourages them by the promise of success. All the seeds from His hand did not come to harvest (was not Judas one of the Twelve ?) ; and the disciple is not above his Master. S. Paul was almost a total failure at Athens. The Word has to be sown—that is the business of the Church and its members ; the conditions of success are in the soil.

(3) THE SOIL is not uniform throughout the field, as is shown sooner or later by its various reception of, and response to, the Seed.

> (a) There are paths across the unfenced field packed hard by frequent feet, so hard that the scattered seed lies exposed upon the surface. The soil cannot " take it in," and soon the passing foot or keen-eyed bird destroys it. It never begins to live ; it never germinates ; it fails in Spring.
>
> (b) Here and there a crumbling stony edge appears, telling of shelving rock below, lightly covered with soil. *So far as it goes* this soil is quite good, but there is not enough of it. For a time the seed does well, it makes a good start and the braird looks healthy, but the growing rootlets cannot strike down : the bottom is too hard. The Summer sun sucks

all the moisture from the shallow earth, and the little stalks wilt and die. The heat that ought to have made for life and growth has made for death, because there is a deficiency of root. The seed germinates but does not grow ; it fails in Summer.

(c) In some places which have not been thoroughly cleaned lie hidden seeds of Nature's sowing. They spring up with the good seed, but they are there first and have an advantage. They hurt the young corn-plants in two ways : by exhausting the soil of nourishment which they should have had, and by their rapid growth overshadowing the corn and shutting off the sunlight. So the ear remains thin and green, it never ripens ; it fails in Autumn.

(d) Throughout the rest of the field the seed germinates, grows and ripens. Even here there are differences, for some parts are more fertile than others, and the seeds in the ear vary very much in number—some a hundred-fold, some sixty, some thirty—yet in all there is the joy of harvest. The sown seed is returned many times over.

II. Reaping.

The basal thought is that the success and failure of the Gospel depend upon the *conditions under which it is received*. Everywhere the soil is intended for the seed and seems to have the possibility of growth and harvest, but it is not all equally prepared for it :

some parts want breaking up, others deepening, others cleaning ; the rest is ready. So the Gospel varies in its results with men—not because the soil is bad—*i.e.*, not because some men are evil, but because men receive it under more or less favourable conditions. These different conditions are present from the first, at the time of receiving, although their effects show themselves at different times later on. The sympathy of the soil to the seed is tested by experience : time is the revealer.

The success of the Christian Life is conditioned by its reception. Spring conditions Harvest : Youth determines Age. Man becomes openly what he is secretly : Will, Conscience and Heart *now* are determining the future.

(*A*) There are those who hear the word and do not " take it in." This is not from vice or folly or misunderstanding—they know that words are seeds— there is simply non-reception. They are impassive, negligent, heedless. For all they care the seeds might be gravel : the Gospel might be in an unknown tongue. It never gets into them at all : their ears get it, not their hearts.

How do men thus keep out what is directly intended for them ? *They are otherwise occupied ;* they are dense to the Evangel because busy with passing, petty things, as the tracks were hardened by many passing feet. They are too open to the gossip and commonplaces of the day to be sensible of finer issues ; they are preoccupied. There they sit in church, but the words read and preached go no further than the ear ; they remain impassive, uninterested, intent on other things—their neighbours and their friends, home and lovers, business and amusements—deaf to the one thing needful, missing their chance. When they leave, any trifling thing—a vagrant word, a flying rumour—removes what is lying on the surface of memory. Worldly preoccupation means spiritual barrenness : it is the tragedy of the commonplace. " Who hath ears to hear, let him *hear*."

(*B*) Others hear the word sympathetically, even emotionally, yet its life in them is of the briefest. They receive it with joy, but are not rooted and grounded, so that at the first hot touch of trial or tongue of criticism their spiritual promise withers away. The message has not gripped the conscience and the will ; their heart of hearts is hard, not " broken and contrite." Such are the emotionalists and mere sentimentalists who go little further than the enquiry room or the Confirmation Class. The gracious promise of the soul shown there gets withered by the discouragement of friends, the scorching laugh of companions, the atmosphere of worldly surroundings. There is no depth of character, to let patience have her perfect work. There is nothing behind and beneath, and such spiritual precocity is a dangerous thing. Plants with long tap-roots stand drought best ; grass withers early.

Religion which is *only* Emotion and Thrill cannot endure : it needs Sympathy, Conscience, Intellect and Will—the whole man. Then contempt and disfavour send one back to strike deep into the sustaining powers of Divine grace ; what withers the emotionalist gives the thoughtful Christian a richer knowledge of his Lord. The Christian Life must be deep before it can be lofty and strong : Christianity without character and depth of purpose is a failure.

(*C*) As unripe grain is of no use in harvest, so a Christian Life which never matures is a disappointment. Such a life comes from a want of complete consecration, absence of whole-hearted service ; the fruits of the Spirit are lacking. The Church knows these too well : in the pews they are the burden of the preacher's soul, in the pulpit they mean spiritual powerlessness. Faithful in outward observance they are of no profit to Christ and His Causes : even in life's Autumn they lack the ripe sweetness of complete devotion.

Here Religion has not gripped the whole man, perhaps does not take even first place with him. Things alien to Christ have been permitted to grow alongside. The resources of life are being largely exhausted on earthly and easy, natural interests ; the soul is choked by too many endeavours. " Busy here and there," the best has gone. Such men want Christ sincerely but not thoroughly ; they allow other wants to prevail also. The simplicity which ought to be toward Him is lacking ; when He claims first place and last place He gets only *a* place. A divided soul is fruitless for Christ. No man can serve two masters : " this one thing I do " is the only way.

The usual interests inimical to Christ are " the cares of the world, and the deceitfulness of riches, and the lusts of other things " : our cares, our comforts and our covetings ; our worries, our wealth and our wants ; poverty, possession and passion—*i.e.*, worldliness, the constant enemy of Christian perfection and fruitfulness.

1. The first of these is dangerous to the spiritual life of the masses : anxiety about ways and means. Poverty is no evil (who was poorer than the homeless Jesus ?) ; Worry is. Having little of earthly riches, men may miss the unsearchable riches in forgetting that He careth for them. Care is the enemy of Faith. An over-anxious parent should remember that God is at least as good a Father as he is. Religion flourishes more in a peasantry than in the crowded tenements and city slums : life is less worried and care-full.

2. The second threatens the well-to-do. The deceitfulness of riches lies in their lulling power of comfort. Some rich men were better and happier when they were poorer ; they have lost more—and richer—than they have gained. Money may fence life : it is no part of life. The pleasant things it procures can sap the spiritual strength. Comfort, Respectability and Fashion—desired for themselves—lessen the spiritual power and output of an individual or a church.

3. The last includes all wants which have not the will of God in them : the present pride of muscle and intellect, selfish desires, unconsecrated ambitions, unhallowed loves ; all that is desired for the ends of self-gratification, all that divides the field of life with Christ. This searches the human heart in all its strange devisings and desires.

As the seeds which choked the growing corn were there before the sowing, so these spiritual enemies are *natural, easy, familiar*. They are in us all, perhaps unsuspected, until we find them conflict with Christ. The inner life needs watching and weeding. It takes time to be holy. Religion means concentration. " Create in me a *clean* heart, O God." A Christian must be neither an amateur nor a dilettante : love to God is with *all* our heart and soul and strength and mind. It is not Christ *and*, but Christ *or*, the world. The works of the flesh are easy : the fruits of the Spirit need time and care.

(*D*) Like good soil, soft, deep and clean, the soul that bears fruit unto God is willing, sincere and thorough ; it receives the word with sympathy, is searched by it to the very depths, and makes God's glory its chief end. And thus the hoped-for harvest comes : the test of the faithful Christian is his life.

Yet even here there are differences—the hundred-fold and sixty-fold of S. John and Augustine and Bunyan, the thirty-fold of the faithful in every age. But the difference is in amount, not in kind, for the seed was the same, and so is the fruit. There is harvest in all, that is the great matter—harvest which satisfies the Sower's eye and heart.

. . . .

What will you do with the good seed of this Parable ? It is sown for you while you read the Scripture passage : is it sown in your heart ? What will the harvest be ? Present conditions—the conditions of reading or of hearing *now*, determine your return to the Lord of the Harvest. In which class of the four have you set yourself ?

THE SOWER AND THE SEED

or,

THE SECRET ORDER OF SPIRITUAL
GROWTH.

S. MARK, iv. 26-29.

THOUGH given by only one Evangelist this little
Parable seems a necessary sequel to the great Parable
of the Sower and the Soil. It dealt with Sowing;
this deals with Growing. The one gives the relation
of the Soil to the Seed; this gives the relation of the
Sower to the Seed. It is the Life-story of the Seed
in Good Soil. As the farmer waits, so Christ waits;
so must all preachers and teachers wait.

(I) WAITING.—After sowing the farmer does nothing more to the seed; he does not worry over it;
his nightly rest remains unbroken so far as it is concerned. He can only wait and watch; he cannot
affect the seed, and is no longer responsible for its
growth. "The law that shuts the seed out from us,
shuts it in with God." He trusts in the soil and his
preparation of it, and in the inherent vitality of the
seed. He cannot interfere with nature and with life,
but he waits and watches, for he knows that harvest
will come.

(2) MYSTERY.—Life—Germination and Growth—is a Mystery: " he knoweth not how." He is positive as to the fact, without understanding it. The seed *will* develop: how and precisely when are beyond him. All life is a mystery whether in a wheat-seed or in a human soul. The living word of God is a new power introduced into the heart, secret and Divine. " The mystery of the life of God in any and in every heart is unfathomable ; and all attempts to determine its course can only work mischief." Cf. also S. John, iii. 8.

(3) ORDER.—The farmer knows that there must be a slow Process of Ordered Growth. There is a sequence to be followed, which he cannot affect ; there is the Law of the Life of the growing seed and plant. This succession—" blade," " ear," " full corn "—must take place. Here is the main lesson of the Parable.

Only ignorance or folly expects Harvest to succeed at once to Sowing. This gradual growth along definite lines is inevitable. " Sanctification is the *work* of God's free grace." A convert is as perfect as a newly germinated seed or a young plant, but to expect the ripe fruits of the Christian Life, Experience and Service there is to be disappointed, and to experiment with souls along these lines will only wound and check them. However the Christian Life in the soul comes it must never be forgotten that it is only the *beginning* of Christian Experience : the one is a fact, the other is a process. Many Christian lives may no more merit reproof or criticism than an undeveloped corn-plant may be blamed for unripeness : both are on the way. They are incomplete, not imperfect. This is conspicuously true of converts in non-Christian lands.

(4) HOPE.—He knows also that growth is slow. He must neither worry nor hurry. Health of spirit, like health of body, is " just the development of the whole nature in its due sequence and proportions." A mushroom grows more quickly than an acorn ; the higher the existence the slower the maturity. Who shall define the time of a soul's maturity ?

Present Imperfections ought not to discourage the preacher and teacher. The harvest is sure if he is true, but he cannot reap in May.

(5) HARVEST.—But he knows that Harvest will come so he can well afford to wait. His activity in the field is resumed at the time of Reaping : between these actions he has been practically powerless. His effort in sowing has been his best ; his trust in the Divine goodness is sure : and God honours both. " He giveth the increase." The faithful preacher leaves results to God.

The Christian Harvest is seen in Saintly Lives, Generosity and Sacrifice, Christian Patience, a Happy Heart and a Bright Smile, Willing and Devoted Service. It is seen in Social Changes, National Revolutions, Cleaner and Higher Standards of Life. It will be found in individuals, churches and nations. Every Christian idea and truth is a seed which shall one day be harvested.

Harvest is a visible thing. The Christian Life begins in getting and ends in giving. God sends the seed into your heart : what will He harvest when He comes to reap ?

THE MUSTARD SEED AND
THE LEAVEN

or,

THE SURPRISING FUTURE OF THE
KINGDOM OF GOD.

S. MATTHEW, xiii. 31, 32.   S. MATTHEW, xiii. 33.
S. MARK, iv. 30-32.   S. LUKE, xiii. 18, 19.   S. LUKE, xiii. 20, 21.

THESE Parables are full of Hope ; there is Promise
and Potency in them.   The Sower meets with disappointments ;   the Growing Seed speaks only of
certainty, not of extent ;   the Tares tell of admixture
and fraud :   but these speak of *future greatness*, how
it is scarcely possible to put limits to one's expectancy
in the spread of the Kingdom of God.   The end is
out of all proportion to the beginning.

THE MUSTARD SEED.

This was proverbial (cf. S. Luke, xvii. 6) for its
smallness, being one of the very tiniest familiar to
gardeners, but it produced a shrub perhaps ten feet
high and big enough for birds to perch upon.   The bush
was out of all proportion to the seed.   The difference
between the acorn and the oak is not so great.

22

THE LEAVEN.

Indoors the house-mother sets a little piece of leaven into the heart of a large quantity of dough, and soon the hidden fermentation affects the whole, permitting of its being baked for food. It seems a large effect from a small cause. " A practically indefinite quantity of flour so treated can be leavened by ' a little leaven.' "

(1) OPTIMISM.—The modest terms in which the Gospel is described—the tiny seed, the little leaven— meet the feeling of even the most despondent disciple : the Gospel, if worth anything at all, cannot be set forth in less terms than these.

It also warns against despising the day of small things : spiritual life is rich in potency. Principles are Prophecies ; Truths make History ; Ideas work Revolutions and Reformations. In the beginning there may be only a " Word."

The modesty of the similes used only emphasises the Assurance and Greatness of His Expectation : His Gospel, He quietly affirms, will succeed with a success in striking contrast with the present. The Gospel of the lonely Jesus will cover the earth as the waters cover the sea. The Death upon the Cross is the irresistible Claim to the Crown.

Note.—Are the words " the birds lodge in the branches " merely additional description of the size attained by the shrub, or have they a parabolic value ? If the latter, the meaning may be that those who once would have devoured the seed are glad later on of its shelter. The Church has Blessing even for those not of its own body.

(2) PROPHECY.—(*a*) The Mustard Seed becoming a tree suggests The Kingdom of God as an ORGANISATION, the visible growth of the Church. History is the best comment : the Cross surmounts the crowns of emperor and king, and the voice of Christian Praise is never silent. The Galilean is triumphing. In face of the facts no Christian dare be a pessimist. Every Christian Mission is like another seed of mustard : it doth not yet appear what it shall be. Faith sees the tree while it plants the seed.

(*b*) The Leaven working in the meal suggests The Kingdom of God as an INFLUENCE, an invisible pervasive power in human society. This is the Christianising of men, as the former is their Evangelising. Beneath the surface of society the *ferment* of Christian ideas and principles is working with amazing results at last in social change and moral advance—*e.g.*, Slavery and Purity. Think of India. Christianity is intensive as well as extensive. Ideas are explosive and disruptive things.

(3) GRACE.—The gardener " took " the seed ; the housewife " took " the leaven : they were there already. They were not made by them ; they were but the agents to give them their opportunity. Christianity is God-given but man-operated. The Gospel is ours by the Divine Grace, yet we must act, that others may know that gracious Gospel also. In giving us the increase God is giving fresh seed and new power. George Eliot says, " All fruit is seed."

The Power of Christianity for growth and expansion is the surprise and satisfaction of humanity. We are on the winning side, and in the Sign of the Cross we conquer. Ninian at Candida Casa and Columba in Iona were insignificant and unknown in a remote corner of Europe : what of the Church of Scotland to-day in this and other lands ?

THE WHEAT AND THE TARES

or,

THE TOLERATION OF EVIL IN THE KINGDOM OF GOD.

S. MATTHEW, xiii. 24-30, 36-43.

JESUS does not conceal from His disciples the troubles which will afflict the Church. The Parable is a forecast of the future.

THE STORY.—A well-sown field when nearing harvest is found to be infested with a plant whose seeds are hurtful and dangerous to man. In its earlier stages its resemblance to wheat prevented its detection. The farmer had sown good seed : whence, then, came this ? It had been the secret night-work of an enemy. So closely, however, are the wheat and tares growing together, that to attempt plucking out the latter by hand will only injure the former, so the separation is left until the harvest, when the bad stuff is bundled up for burning and the good put safely in the barn.

INTERPRETATION AND LESSON.—The interpretation is given by the Master Himself in great detail : vv. 36-43.

26

(1) It is important to notice here that the Seed is not the Word sown in the heart, but the *members of the Kingdom themselves :* it is not sown *in* man ; it *is* man. In the Parable of the Sower the evil influences whose presence hurts the good seed are in the human heart : here it is a rival crop in the field of the world, whose removal will hurt the wheat. This Parable is concerned with false, not faulty, Christians ; not with deficient and inefficient members of the Kingdom, but with pseudo-members, counterfeits. Their falsity is proved by their conduct, for it is at the time of "fruit" (v. 26) that the deceit becomes apparent.

This Parable is "more abstruse than the Sower, its lesson deeper, the facts it points to more mysterious." Towards the close it introduces us to a mysterious spirit-world, with the devil and angels, a furnace and a glory, rendering interpretation difficult.

On the assumption that the "servants" of the story are the Ministry of the Church, opinion has varied as to how far it permits Church Discipline and Excommunication—*e.g.*, is it permissible when the evil is limited in extent, but not when it is scattered over the whole field, or is it entirely forbidden ? It seems preferable to confine ourselves to the broad teachings of the story.

(2) There is a clear *warning against expectation of a perfect world*. The Mustard Seed was a very modest statement of the present : this warns us against too sanguine a view of the future. And this, even while Jesus calls that world "His Kingdom" (v. 41). The sons of the "evil one" will always be found commingled with the "sons of the kingdom" ; there are diabolic forces at work producing many Christian

shams, frauds and counterfeits. When, after the sowing of good seed, we look for a wheat crop only, we shall find much that is quite the reverse. Jesus expects on earth no perfect Church, and History has ratified the Parable from Judas, Ananias and Demas down to the latest scandal of some hypocritical church member. Enthusiasts may wish for Utopias and perfect institutions, but Jesus here arms His Church against disappointments. He does not justify the existence of any evil in the Kingdom of God, but He says that surprise at its presence is uncalled for. No matter how faithful the Church may be to sow, the devil is at least as busy at the same work, but with very different seed !

(3) *The Removal of the Counterfeit is forbidden.*—The Master's policy is Waiting. Whatever evil the Church may show—and at times the good has been far to seek—the cure is not the outcasting of men. It is bigotry to persecute ; it is Pharisaism to withdraw oneself. Judas was allowed to remain, even when the Master knew how he stole from the common purse. The evil which appears in the Church does not necessarily mean negligence : the tares were sown when men had betaken themselves to natural and necessary sleep (v. 25).

This *Waiting is for the sake of the Wheat.* The servants are concerned at the presence of the tares ; their Master is concerned that the wheat shall not suffer by their meddling. Weeding will only hurt the good, He says. To unchurch men offends tender, honest souls ; persecution and excommunication weaken the Church.

(4) Jesus commands *Patience, not Plucking*, Waiting,

28

not Wasting, Faith, not Fury. The field is the world : is it yet all sown ? Let the weeding alone. Not Censure but Service is our duty. Let men labour and wait, knowing that the Ultimate Saving of the Good is sure, and equally sure is the Ultimate Destruction of the Sham. The enemy may give no little trouble, but he is beaten at the last. One day God will save and own His own.

(5) The immediate question is : *what are we ?* Wheat or tares ? Christ's work or the devil's ? How shall we be classed in the harvest ? The picture of the end is somewhat awesome : annihilation or preservation. Sham Christians will be shown to be so, and will be discarded by Jesus.

How could any minister begin to search his congregation and divide them into classes ? Would he not make many mistakes and do only harm ? What he considered tares might be but imperfect, deficient, yet struggling Christians. What he considered decent wheat might be but tares whose evil fruit had not manifested itself as yet.

The essential is : what are we ? On whose side ? What is our spiritual kinship ?

Note.—A kindred and helpful inquiry might be made under this Parable as to—

(1) The proper attitude to, and treatment of, erroneous and heretical opinion in the Church ;
(2) The effectiveness or otherwise of an '' Index Expurgatorius '' ; and
(3) The Church's attitude to questionable and poisonous literature.

THE DRAG-NET

or,

THE ULTIMATE SEPARATION OF GOOD FROM EVIL IN THE KINGDOM OF GOD.

S. MATTHEW, xiii. 47-50.

THE instruction of this Parable is much like that of The Wheat and The Tares. Its sphere is the sea, and its action fishing, but the parallelism of meaning is clear.

THE STORY.—When a seine-net is paid out into the sea in a great semicircle and then dragged ashore, all kinds of fish will appear : large and small, alive and dead, edible and unwholesome. (The contents of a modern trawl are a wonder to a landsman.) But the time for sorting them is not while pulling the net, but when the fishing is over. So it is the Church's duty now to be fishers of men : God will separate in His own time. The separation will be thorough and deliberate ; they " sat down " to it.

LESSONS.—As before there are here—

(1) The certainty of good and bad in the visible Kingdom of God : popular movements bring all kinds of people together.

(2) The mistake made if separation is attempted at once : it is really an impossibility while fishing.

(3) The necessity of leaving the bad alone for a time, the time fixed being the end of the fishing.

(4) The assurance of the ultimate retention of the good and the destruction of the worthless. All are fish, but all are not good fish.

(5) Is our life poisonous or wholesome ?

II.

THE
WORTH OF THE KINGDOM

THE FOUND TREASURE AND
THE PRECIOUS PEARL

or,

THE SURPRISING VALUE OF THE KINGDOM
OF GOD.

S. MATTHEW, xiii. 44-46.

WHAT are the feelings and actions of an individual
when he sees the Kingdom of Heaven open to him ?
In the Parables dealing with Sowing and Growing,
the Soil, *i.e.,* the Receiver, is necessarily treated as a
passive thing ; here we have the activities of the
recipient : the effect of the Gospel upon a heart that
sees and appreciates how personal contact with God
moves and inspires. *It comes as something worth every
endeavour to secure.*

FOUND TREASURE.

In a land where property was insecure through
misrule or invasion Treasure was frequently concealed
or buried in a cave, a sepulchre, a field, until the
immediate danger had passed. But death or exile

35

might prevent the owner from ever possessing his wealth again, so his hoard would remain buried and unknown. Long afterwards a farm labourer comes across it, and is dazzled by seeing a fortune within his grasp. Concealing it again and keeping silence, he turns *all he has*—his furnishings and household gods—into cash, and secures that field by purchase. The honesty of the finder is not before us ; in more than one Parable our Lord finds illustration of that which is highest in that which is low—*e.g.*, the Unjust Judge and Steward. What He gives are simply pictures of what might happen any day in Palestine.

THE PRECIOUS PEARL.

In the ancient world the pearl was the most highly prized jewel, and merchants sought them from India to Britain, sure of a market for fine specimens. Cleopatra possessed two worth £80,000 each ; Cæsar gave to Servilia, mother of Brutus, one valued at £48,000 ; and Augustus dedicated to Jupiter Capitolinus jewels and pearls worth £400,000. Such a travelling merchant is one day offered a pearl excelling any he has ever seen ; it is indeed so fine that all he carries with him cannot purchase it ; it was quite beyond experience or expectation that he should ever be offered such. Knowing its value, however, he determines to secure it, and so sells *all he has*—his stock of jewels and other property—to make it his own. Things he once treasured now count for nothing, if only he can secure this. With it he knows he is made for life, for it will bring him a fortune.

The central thought of both stories is the same ; the differences will be noted in passing.

(1) In both cases there is DISCOVERY : the word " found " is used of both. They are confronted with what they are not looking for : Hidden Treasure and a Unique Pearl. Though he is a seeker the Merchant was quite unprepared for such a pearl as this ; this find is beyond his dreams. The one has the surprise and " joy " of *Treasure Trove ;* the other the surprise and pleasure of *Perfection.* What they find is quite familiar ; there is nothing strange about coin to the one and pearls to the other ; but their richness is entirely unexpected.

The Kingdom of God comes to the soul that sees and appreciates it as a surprise, a delight, a treasure, something unique, which must be secured : it were folly to miss the chance. God—*for oneself*—is a discovery, yet one quickly and thoroughly grasped. God is not a stranger ; Religion is not unnatural : it is the crown of life's desire. It is the peace and joy of humanity at their best. To possess God is life's perfect satisfaction. He answers the deepest longings of the soul ; the Gospel fits us and settles us. There is nothing like God elsewhere ; to experience Him is unique. He has made us for Himself, and our souls cannot find rest until they rest in Him.

(2) Both men are determined to secure their finds, and the measure of their determination is their THOROUGHNESS : both sell " *all* " that they have. They do not feel they are making any sacrifice—quite the reverse ; they are going to be richer than they

ever were before ; they are getting far more than they
are giving. They are acting in a most business-like
fashion : to increase your capital enormously without
risk in a few hours is not a sacrifice !

Whether as a sudden Discovery, or as the Culmina-
tion of all life's desires, The Kingdom of Heaven is the
same—the *summum bonum* which is worth more than
all else. Christ and His Gospel, the Love of the Father,
and the Blessing of His Grace, are the Best the soul
can ever attain ; and when the soul suddenly recognises them *for what they are*—entirely fitted to enrich
one for ever—nothing is permitted to stand in the
way of making them its own. There is no sense of
sacrifice but only of gain, in *making sure of God*.
Read S. Paul's opinion of Christ in the Epistle to the
Philippians, iii. 7-8.

(3) The Gospel is a thing of GRACE. It comes un-
looked-for, unearned, unexpected. This note is
repeated frequently in the Parables. The poor in
spirit, the sinful soul, the publican and the Magdalene,
thrills with joy at the rich possibilities which Christ
suddenly opens up ; such a mercy is altogether unlooked for : while the thinker, the poet, the artist,
he whose life is occupied with fair and beautiful
thoughts and things, sees in Christ also something far
beyond his dreams, something he must possess or he
will never know peace of mind or happiness again.

Both men have found a fortune : the Poor Man is
now Rich, and the Scholar is at last Wise ! The
world has nothing to offer—to sinner or to saint, to
ignorance or to knowledge—like the Gospel of Jesus
Christ.

THE GREAT SUPPER AND
ITS GUESTS

or,

THE RECEPTION OF GOD'S KINGDOM
BY THE SATISFIED AND THE NEEDY.

S. LUKE, xiv. 15-24.

THE OCCASION.—This is an example of how the
Lord's Parables were sometimes elicited by the words
of others, and how He found His similes in the events
of the moment. It had its occasion at a dinner, and
it deals with a feast. It is really a bit of His table-
talk as the guest of a Pharisee one Sabbath Day.[1]

He has noted the behaviour of the other guests
seeking the more prominent places in the room, and
He counsels them to the very opposite. He softens
the criticism somewhat by referring it to a future
invitation to something special like a marriage banquet, but points out that to seat oneself in a good
place was to incur the risk of humiliation in being
asked to vacate it for some more important but later
arrival, whereas choosing a less conspicuous place may

[1] It is worth noting that the Jewish Sabbath Day Feast
was a " cold collation."

39

lead to the conspicuous honour of being asked to come up higher. The Parable which follows a little later is an example of many getting a very unexpected invitation.

Turning to His host He suggests in a semi-humorous fashion that there is danger in the practice of entertaining only one's relatives and rich friends—the danger of having to accept invitations from all of these in turn ! Such hospitality is unreal : real hospitality is to entertain persons who are too poor to give anything in return ; it means blessing to them now, and to the host hereafter. The proper use of wealth and power is to ends which have nothing of self in them ; Philanthropy is better than Ambition : it is a finer thing to be a host at the table of life than to be the guest of the great. To use one's leisure in teaching children about God, one's talents for music or art in brightening some dark and narrow lives, one's house or garden for the lonely student, the invalid and the slum-worker, is "twice blest ; It blesseth him that gives and him that takes." A Church which lives for itself and not for the outcast, the ignorant and the poor, is starving its own soul. There are no millionaires buried in Westminster Abbey : men who served and gave are there.

Jesus finished His smiling advice to His host with the words, "at the resurrection of the just," and this leads one of the guests to say : "Blessed is he that shall eat bread in the Kingdom of God ! " The Jewish conception of the future blessedness took the somewhat material form of a banquet. Whether this exclamation is a piece of pious cant, thought suitable to the occasion and to the Guest of the day, or a longing, wistful and entirely sincere remark, is not easily decided. The fact that the Master at once speaks a Parable to point out that men are not really so keen on the Kingdom of God as they profess, inclines one to the former view : He makes a story to correct him.

THE STORY.—A gentleman is planning to entertain his friends at a large supper-party, and many invited guests have accepted. At the appointed time a servant is sent, in accordance with custom, to tell them that all is ready, but not one of them finds it convenient to attend, and each has a reason for absence which seems good enough to him. The disappointed host is so indignant that he sends out to the city lanes and slums for any and every poor and unfortunate person who can be found, and when there is still room others are swept in from yet farther away, from the rural roads and hedge-sides, for he is determined that the house shall be filled, and that these indifferent friends shall get no chance of consuming what they have treated so casually.

THE APPLICATION.—As an event of actual experience the story is scarcely credible. For *every* guest to decline is a most unlikely thing : is He not at that very moment at a table where the guests were pressing to the chief places ? But this improbability gives the sting to the tale. This, says Jesus, is how men really treat the Invitation of God : they care less for Him and His than for their own interests. They are not so intent on the blessings of the Future Life as the other speaker implied : this present life suffices them. The

Lord knew only too well how the leaders of the nation and the professedly religious were receiving Him Who came to announce that the Kingdom of God was waiting for them ; they were too self-satisfied and self-righteous to feel any interest, still less a keenness which would throw everything else to one side, in Him and His Mission. What though their profession as loyal Jews implied obedience to the Will of God and a promise to serve Him ? He does not find them in the least sympathetic, but rather critical to the verge of hostility; He does not see them coming gladly to the Kingdom, its welcome and its gracious bounty. The only persons who seem to be prepared to show any keenness and interest are despised outsiders, "the publicans and sinners," the waifs and wastrels of society. The common people are hearing Him gladly, coming readily to the Table of the Divine Love.

With the coming of Christ the hour of God's Feast had come, but the first-invited guests with one consent turned from it, even though they were pledged as God's people. A generation later, when Paul was refused a hearing by the Jews, he turned to the Gentiles, and they became the guests of God. The improbability of the Parable is painfully true of the Kingdom.

THE LESSONS.—These are two : a *Criticism of Man* for his shortsightedness in the things of God and the soul, and a Declaration of the *Graciousness of God*.

(1) *Of Man*. The invited guests prefer their own concerns to the Feast, in spite of their promise. They were *expected*, but at the last moment failed. Their

reasons were legitimate and probably true, but they were pretexts, not valid reasons. The newly purchased farm would not spoil by another night's delay, and the trial of the team could easily be put off till to-morrow, while even a bride would not begrudge her man the honour of supping with an important person. These three are given as samples, not to be regarded as exhaustive. All had considered it worth while to promise, and not one of them says " I forgot " ; but where there is no will there is a stay-away. They did not want to go when it came to the point ; their personal interests seemed of greater importance. The excuses given are quite suitable to the occasion of a supper, but it was none of these which kept the Jewish leaders from believing on Jesus : it was what they considered their personal interests bound up with their theological conceptions of the Kingdom and its material glory, so different from the words of this humble Carpenter of Nazareth. There is no positive sin ascribed to the refusing guests ; their fault is that of *pre-occupation and indifference*. Their private affairs cannot wait, they think ; so the host must wait for them in vain. In spite of their promise he takes the second place.

Thus the Master suggests to us the inclination of men to *make God secondary* : second to personal and physical concerns. They may talk about their relation-ship with Heaven, yet their engagement with God is forgotten when something of individual moment arises ; they are not really serious in their religion. There are those who make a Christian Profession, but have never had a definite meeting with God and know nothing of spiritual joy and true communion with the Father. They treat God lightly ; they are easily turned away from Him. They are not really so intent on His company as appearance and language suggest. When God invites, man must do more than accept—he must *go*. First things must come first ; and the first thing for a child of God is the Will of God, in whatever strange or unwelcome experience it may come. It must be done on earth as the angels do it in heaven : at once, without asking any questions.

The sample excuses are suggestive. There is Property, which speaks of Land and Pride and Ambition, a parallel to " the deceitfulness of riches " in The Sower ; there is the new team of Oxen, telling of Business and Industry, " the cares of the world " ; and there is the Bride, warning us how Home and Comfort, " the desires of other things," may affect to lower levels the life of the soul. Generally, they suggest that things in themselves innocent may make a man lose the Best when the issue is the direct call of God to the individual. To neglect God is the supreme folly.

Lord Chancellor Cairns gave testimony that if he had had any success in life it was due to the fact that the first two hours of the day were given to the Word of God and to Prayer. Questioned as to this, his widow said : " I do not know about the two hours, but I know this, that no matter how late he went to bed at night he always got up at the same hour every morning (it was 6.30) for prayer and Bible-study." God first : " in the beginning, God."

In Collingwood's ' Life of John Ruskin ' (Book IV., Chapter 3) will be found the narrative of a lady who refused him in marriage, because he could not say that he loved God more than her. Even when near her end he still said " No," so " her door was closed upon him for ever."

(2) *Of God*. This is a Parable of the Amazing Sweep of the Divine Grace. It is a declaration of the Divine Will, and a defence of the Lord's action reflecting that Will, in preaching to the publicans and sinners. It shares with others in its attractive presentation of the Kingdom. The Master presents it under most alluring images, that man may be drawn from sordid and materialistic love to seek that which is the true enrichment and enhancement of life. It is likened to Found Treasure, to a Pearl of Peerless Beauty, to the Marriage-Feast of a Prince. Here we have it likened to a Supper—a Great Supper—that to which men are invited ; something given, not earned ; of grace, not of merit. The spirit of the host is found in his resolve that the outcast and the poor shall get their places at his table. Nothing less than a full house will content him, and so those who think that such an invitation is too good to be true are to be constrained to come in. Such large-heartedness is a worthy emblem of the magnificence of Divine Grace and the Waiting Welcome of a Heavenly Father. " Both Nature and Grace abhor a vacuum," says Bengel. There is no privilege in the Kingdom of God : or rather, it is *all* privilege : " Whosoever will, may come."

One word alone *seems* harsh (v. 24), but it is from the offended host it comes, not from Jesus. It is part of the story, remember. Beware of ascribing his indignation to the Father. It was not because the Jewish Leaders refused Jesus that He went to the publicans and sinners, but because His message of the Divine Heart was too catholic for the former; as Paul also turned to the Gentiles, only when the wideness of the Gospel was too wide for the mind of the synagogue. "The grace went before the indifference, and was its cause, not its effect" (Bruce). The ethics of a Parable are not necessarily the ethics of the Kingdom of God; and the dominant of this Parable is Grace, not Judgment. Yet even at its lowest level the action of the host is that of a magnanimous man, of generous and charitable instincts, with a noble indignation, which knows no malice or meanness; and if man's indignation leads to such kindness, to what will the Divine Charity not lead!

So the Parable rings with the limitless goodness of God; His Kingdom is for the Hungry who appreciate it, not for the satisfied and Selfishly Occupied who prefer other things. It has nothing in it of merit or desert, only of need. The host is pleased when the house is full, and the guests are satisfied when they have believed the invitation and have come. God's blessings are for those who do care. "God bestoweth His blessings there, where He findeth the vessels empty." The Kingdom of Heaven is for those who have need: all Missions and Missionary Work are in this story. God wishes to see men happy, to have no vacant places at the Table of His Love.

> "For a cap and bells our lives we pay,
> Bubbles we buy with a whole soul's tasking;
> 'Tis Heaven alone that is given away,
> 'Tis only God may be had for the asking."

THE MARRIAGE-SUPPER OF THE KING'S SON AND THE GUEST WITHOUT A WEDDING-GARMENT

or,

THE REJECTED RESPONSIBILITY ALIKE OF PRIVILEGE AND GRACE.

S. MATTHEW, xxii. 1-14.

THE substance and purpose of the main Parable closely resemble those of The Great Supper, which should be carefully compared (p. 39). Comparison with that of The Unfaithful Husbandmen is also advisable (p. 72).

THE STORY.—A feast has been arranged by a king in honour of the marriage of his son, and the festivities are to extend over several days. Servants are sent to call the invited guests, but they will not come. Others are sent, adding to the invitation attractive details of the richness and preparedness of the entertainment, but even this is fruitless. They treat the invitation very lightly, and go about their affairs, farming, business and so on. Some abuse and actually kill the messengers. This is more than selfish rudeness; there is rebellion and treason in it. The angry king then sends messengers of another sort:

47

soldiers who put the unworthy guests to death and burn up their town. Thereafter servants are sent to where the country roads come together near the city gates, with instructions to bring in all they meet, regardless of character, and soon the tables are full. We picture to ourselves the motley happy throng, delighted with this unexpected treat.

THE INTERPRETATION.—This is along the lines of Jewish History. That nation is the invited company, the favoured and chosen people, who refuse to recognise the call of God given by His servants, the prophets. Worldly affairs seem of more worth than sitting at the Table of God. Their next call, from John the Baptist and Jesus Himself, that the day had come, is also neglected : nay ! they are abused and slain. Here the story becomes prophecy, telling of the Cross and the destruction of Jerusalem by the Romans in 70 A.D. as punishment for their rebellious and disobedient action. Such was the consequence of the Jewish rejection of Jesus.

The Divine King then sends His invitation far and wide without limitation, as Jesus did to the publican and sinner, and Paul and others did to the Gentile world. After the fall of the Holy City the Gospel message was everywhere proclaimed freely, and accepted by those who had hitherto been regarded as without the pale.

THE LESSONS.—These are as in The Great Supper, but with increased emphasis. The Feast is now in a Royal Palace ; the occasion the joyful one of a Prince's Marriage. Thus the conduct of the invited guests is worse than occupation with personal matters ;

48

there is rebellion and cruelty in it. Their fate is also detailed and dreadful. There is a point in the Divine Economy where Grace gives place to Judgment; there is "the wrath of the Lamb"; opportunity abused is worse than lost.

> " There is a time we know not when,
>   A point we know not where ;
> That marks the destiny of man
>   To glory or despair.
> There is a line by us unseen,
>   That crosses every path,
> The hidden boundary between
>   God's patience and God's wrath."

The graciousness of the host is seen again in the repeated invitation to the first invited, in the lavish feast and—still more—in the wide sweep of the next call, taking in " both bad and good."

The Incident of THE MAN WITHOUT A WEDDING GARMENT is an addition whose truth is also reflected in the lines just quoted. When the royal host visits the happy wondering crowd he finds one who shows by his dress that he has not made the slightest attempt to recognise that he has come to a marriage-feast, still less a royal one. To him the privilege has implied no responsibility. Questioned in a friendly manner by the king he has no explanation to make, and he is cast out into the darkness, to mourn too late his rudeness, folly and want of good feeling. He has come in with the crowd, but has taken the opportunity too lightly. There is an accepted invitation, but there is nothing done.

This has its LESSON for the Gentile world, as the main Parable had for the Jewish. Grace is no excuse

D

for carelessness of life. It suggests the lesson of The Tares and The Net, that in the hour of God's visitation those who have shown by their life an entire want of appreciation of the Blessings of the Fellowship of God will not be found at the Final Feast of the Divine Goodness. Heaven's mercy is not to be treated as commonplace. The branch that bears "no fruit" is taken away. The Gentiles were received into the Church—the House of God—without the restrictions of the Jewish Ritual, but there remained the higher righteousness exceeding that of scribe and Pharisee, the debt to grace, that higher and personal holiness without which no man can see the Lord. (Cf. the Ep. of S. James, ii. 17.) There is but one such offender in the story ; but one is enough to be a warning to all. To become a Christian is to become something *different*—" a new creature " : to attend God's Feast as if it did not matter whether you were there or not will end in your *not being there*. It is God Himself Who is the Judge, asking : Where is your robe of righteousness ; where is the result of your repentance ; where are the fruits of My Spirit ? Favour implies some response : to despise grace is to forfeit it ; Judas goes to his own place.

God has done much for Britain, for us : what is Britain, what are we, doing for God ? The Gentile cannot presume upon the Divine Grace : " if God spared not the natural branches, neither will He spare thee " (Rom., xi. 21).

Notes.

(1) It is possible that the main Parable is the same as that given by S. Luke, told with added emphasis, and with additions from that other which immediately preceded it in

S. Matthew—viz., The Wicked Husbandmen. Their action and their fate are much the same as those of the invited guests.

(2) The allusion to the burning of the city will then be seen as an addition of the Evangelist after the event, showing how the removal of the Jew was a punishment for the Cross and became the opportunity of the Gentile.

(3) The sequence of the various episodes may be thus arranged :—

The Original Invitation.	The Choosing of the Jews.
The first call of the servants.	The call of the prophets.
The second call : " all ready."	The call of the Baptist, Jesus and the Twelve.
The Punishment.	The Fall of Jerusalem.
The General Invitation.	The Preaching to the Gentiles.
The Indifferent Guest.	Unchanged Lives in the Gentile Church.

Some, however, would make the First Call that of John and Jesus, and the Second the Early Preaching of the Apostles.

(4) It seems somewhat unreasonable to expect that guests so hastily assembled from anywhere and everywhere could all make proper preparation for a Feast. (At the same time it should be remembered that it is not " proper " preparation that is in question, so much as *any* preparation.) It has therefore been suggested that this addendum is really a separate Parable, with the Lesson of The Tares and The Drag-Net. If it were introduced by the familiar words, " The Kingdom is likened unto," it would be complete in itself. In that case the words, " both bad and good " (a feature only implied in S. Luke), were inserted when the two were combined into one story, to prepare us for what is coming.

(5) The concluding aphorism, " For many are called, but few are chosen," hangs very loosely to a story which tells of the *many* guests of God. It may be a precious word of the Lord which S. Matthew would not lose, and so appends to a double Parable telling of men who *did lose* their place at the Feast of God.

PATCHING OLD GARMENTS AND PRESERVING NEW WINE

or,

NEW FAITH: NEW FORMS.

S. MATTHEW, ix. 14-17. S. MARK, ii. 18-22. S. LUKE, v. 33-39.

THE OCCASION.—Whether the questioners on this occasion were actually followers of The Baptist and The Pharisees, or others who were familiar with their habits, is not quite clear ; but the probability is the latter. They seem sincerely anxious to understand why the disciples of Jesus differ from these in the practice of Fasting. The question was quite natural, and is received in that spirit, obtaining a full answer from the Master, in " three pregnant parabolic sayings : bright, genial, felicitous impromptus ; the first a happy apology for His disciples, the other two the statement of a general principle " (Bruce). There is a certain gaiety or note of joy in the whole passage.

Fasting, He says, would be most unsuitable for men so full of new spiritual enthusiasm ; they are as happy with Me as a bridegroom's friends at a marriage : and Fasting is the last thing men think of there ! This suggests two things :—

    (1) Jesus' consciousness of His importance for the Life and Joy of His friends : *He* is the Bridegroom in Whom they delight.

(2) There may come seasons in the spiritual life when He seems far away from us—" the bridegroom taken away "—and such a time of broken communion is a call for diligent and rigorous dealing with oneself—a Lenten time.

THE STORIES.—The happiness of a marriage calls up the little Parables which follow, and they deal naturally with the usual accompaniments of such an occasion, clothes and wine. They are stories of what people do *not do*, and are convincing absurdities. Unlike the Parables in general they tell of actions sensible folk abstain from. It is the *argumentum ad absurdum*, for ridiculous things are usually convincing. They are full of geniality and wisdom : the whole passage has His smile in it ; a reflection, perhaps, of the temper of the guests at Levi's table.

To patch an old GARMENT with a piece of unshrunk cloth is to make a bigger hole : as soon as it gets wet it will shrink and tear away part of the old cloth with it. To put a strong new WINE into wine-skins which have been so long used that they have lost all their capacity for stretching, with no more " give " in them, will result in their bursting as soon as the new wine ferments, so that both wine and skins are lost. What are we to learn here ?

APPLICATION.—(1) Jesus and His Message are something *new* for men, and affect society. They are not a Reformed Judaism—the Baptist's Teaching might be that—but a fresh vintage of God, and must be so treated. There is power, vitality, life, in these new ideas He taught ; where He is heard a new day dawns. Thus again He asserts Himself as One Whose words are to be reckoned with and Whose influence is always marked.

(2) Where He comes there comes *change :* old forms and ceremonies will not suit. Old things pass away and all things become new, even man becomes a new creature. Life must be different where Christ is found. New ideas are to be clothed in new garments or habits ; the fresh wine is to be stored in new skins. The Law of Change implies also the Law of Congruity. The new faith, the new attitude to God, will require new forms. This is one reason why the progress of Christianity seems so slow among the old pagan civilisations : it searches life so rigidly, and means so many changes in conduct : it is not a mere form, it is a *Force.* This became very soon quite apparent in the Church, and the record is found in the Book of the Acts and the Letters of S. Paul. The old wine-skins of Judaism could not be used to hold the new Vintage of Christ, in spite of the longings of many Jewish converts. The organism must be modified to meet new conditions ; or, rather, a new organism must appear. The expression of the new Faith seemed madness to some (Cf. i Cor., xiv. 23). (An instructive example of this in the sphere of Religious Architecture will be found in Dr John Watson's volume of Sermons—' The Inspiration of our Faith ' : pp. 160-162.)

(3) To confine the new in the bonds of the old is certain to mean trouble, perhaps *disaster and loss.* In the Middle Ages the tribes of Europe were in many places made nominally Christian by the order of their rulers, and to-day the ancient Pagan customs and

powers are not gone ; Thor has not entirely abdicated to the White Christ, and the Beltane Fires still blaze. There must be change if there is to be progress ; but the true change is within, and it will find its own proper form. To restrain the ferment of new ideas by force means an explosion sooner or later : " Liberty, Equality and Fraternity " become The Terror and The Guillotine.

The Western Church cannot, and does not, expect the Faith of Christ to take in the East or elsewhere precisely the forms it has in Europe ; to think so is just to do what Jesus here says no sane person does ! In the West itself there have been changes : the Shorter Catechism answer to " What is God ? " has neither the word " Father " nor " Love." The researches of Modern Science must be allowed their place in moulding the Creed and Worship of the Church. People must use common sense in Religion, says Jesus ; why is it that so often it comes there last of all ? Change, Congruity and Adaptation are everywhere necessary.

ADDITION.—Perhaps the answer to the last question is here. In the Third Gospel there is a little addition in which the Master sympathetically recognises the conservative mind, which ever tends to say, " The old is better." This instructs the young and forward mind to deal tenderly with the old in their love of tradition and use, while the Parables themselves point out to the lovers of the old that changes are inevitable. The young are no iconoclasts, though they raise what seem rival temples ; nor are the old insincere because they love the ancient shrines.

In this conclusion we have the Master ending on the note of good humour with which He began; there is still a smile upon His face. He knows how difficult it is for the old to welcome the new, after habit is formed and custom fits one like an old coat; but there is a serious warning in the picture of the lost wine, as to the danger of stifling enthusiasm: it may be lost altogether and the world be so much the poorer. " Quench not the Spirit; despise not prophesyings " (I Thess. v. 19-20).

Note.—In S. Luke's account of The Garment and The Patch it seems as if the latter were to be taken from a *new garment.* This " suggests somewhat different ideas, and is by itself by no means clear " (Bruce). It certainly adds to the absurdity of the action.

III.

OUR LORD'S APOLOGIA:
DEFENCE AND ATTACK.

THE DOCTOR'S PLACE

or,

HOW JESUS JUSTIFIES HIS MINISTRY.

S. MATTHEW, ix. 9-13. S. MARK, ii. 13-17. S. LUKE, v. 27-32.

QUITE early in His Ministry our Lord was called upon to justify its form and His audience. The religious of His day found Him followed by a crowd which seemed to them to be most unfitting company for one acting as a Rabbi—" tax-gatherers and sinners " —men with whom no Pharisee would ever associate. Not only was He popular with them but He was actually found at table with them ! This was a new thing to Scribe and Pharisee, and partly in puzzlement and partly in criticism they question His disciples on the matter.

Jesus Himself answered them, and the answer is an " apologia pro vita sua," with a suggested criticism of themselves. His defence is in the proverbial saying about a doctor being required only by people who are ill, and His attack in a quotation from Hosea, as to God caring for mercy rather than sacrifice. (This is found only in S. Matthew's account.)

(1) THE PATIENTS.—He regards these people who were practically outcasted and neglected by the

orthodox as " sinners," no doubt, but as *sinners who may be cured*. They are suffering from sickness of soul, and soreness of heart, shame, remorse and despair, the ailments of the spirit. The cause of these troubles does not affect the fact that they are suffering, and Jesus has found that they are ready to welcome any message or messenger that may restore spiritual vitality and health. " The methods of the prophets, the religion that consists in walking humbly with God, doing justly and loving mercy, can be preached to them with some effect and with good hope of really helping them " (Menzies). He has pity upon them, and it is this pity His critics do not know. Religion is an unselfish and helpful thing, not a selfish matter of position and reputation.

(2) THE PHYSICIAN.—*Jesus regards Himself as a doctor* who can do something for them. He has found that His preaching has comforted and helped many, that the gracious words He spoke were most acceptable and that new hopes and powers were being aroused in them. Surely, then, the proper place for a doctor who has the skill to cure is near the sufferer. That is only common sense ! Power in the hands of Pity must mean Service, if a man has a conscience at all.

(3) THE EVANGEL.—This view of Humanity as suffering from the disease of Sin, and of the Evangel as its cure, is the *justification of all Preaching*, of Missions to the careless and sin-defeated at Home and of Missions to every race under Heaven. In simple speech the Gospel is " good medicine." Wherever there are souls sick from the lack of God

the Christian Message should be sent. This world is in pain, and Christ is the Good Physician. A non-healing Christianity will die.

Note.—If the surprise and criticism of the pious Pharisees surprise us, it is just because we have learned better from Christ. Yet the same critical attitude is very persistent. S. Paul justifies " the foolishness of preaching " in 1 Cor., i. 18 ff. ; towards the close of the second century Celsus was amazed at the efforts of the preachers to make converts " of the silly and senseless, slaves, women, and children," and his attack called forth all the skill and learning of Origen ; Sydney Smith was sarcastic over foreign missionaries as " fanatics " : and there are those " at ease in Zion " to-day who care little or nothing for the misery of sin at home or the want of The Father in pagan lands. But the successes of the Faith have ever been from below upwards, from those who were free from self-interest and convention, from the low-caste and the no-caste folk.

THE LOST SHEEP AND THE LOST SHILLING

or,

THE DIVINE JOY AT RECOVERING THE LOST.

S. MATTHEW, xviii. 12-14. S. LUKE, xv. 1-10.

THREE Parables—The Lost Sheep, The Lost Shilling and The Lost Son—are recorded by S. Luke as being called forth by a critical remark like that which led to the illustration of The Doctor and The Sick Folk. Again the Master justifies His Ministry to tax-gatherer and sinner, and again He turns a Divine mirror towards His critics in which they may see themselves. This time He strikes a higher note ; we hear the music of heaven and the joy of the angels at the recovery of that which was lost. The delight of the owner at recovering what was loved and lost, and the sympathetic pleasure of his friends, are the theme of all three. The joy of heaven explains His Ministry.

An examination of their likenesses and differences is not without interest, but may tend to overmuch allegorising. In all there is Possession, Loss, Search, Recovery, Delight and Sympathetic Joy. The triple

repetition of the lesson emphasises its importance,
and the differences are perhaps no more than necessary
features of the story each tells. There are the witless
sheep, the unconscious coin, the wilful lad ; the
incomplete flock, the disturbed house, the empty
seat ; there is the variety in the numbers—one in a
hundred, one in ten, one in two—but these are only
natural to each picture. Ten sheep are too few to
make the loss of one readily possible, a hundred coins
would have been an unnatural hoard for a village
woman, and two sons suffice to point the moral and
impress the contrast desired. This chapter deals
with only the first two ; the third and greatest is
treated by itself.

(1) NATURAL ACTION.—Jesus defends His Ministry
by an appeal to their own conduct or experience.
" What man of *you* ? " He asks, or " what woman ? "
He finds ample justification for His conduct in the
field and in the home ; the most trivial of life's mis-
fortunes and pleasures are vocal of the will of God.
He finds nothing too common to be used in illustration
of spiritual life.

When people lose things do they not look for
them ? Any man among you will make a very per-
severing search for one of his hundred sheep, and a
woman will sweep her floor well until she find the lost
shilling of her hoard of ten. And are they not glad
when their search is successful ? So glad that they
cannot keep quiet about it, but must have their
friends and neighbours in to tell them the whole
story. " Look, there's the sheep I hunted for ; it's
not a bit the worse, is it ? " " See, here's the money

I missed and found again, none the worse." The number is complete once more, and there is pleasure all round. A coin is a dead thing without feeling, and there is nothing said of the feeling of the wandering sheep—this belongs to the third of the stories—yet it may be noted that no other animal " gives so striking an example of *unrest*, useless expenditure of strength and utter *helplessness* in wandering."

(2) RELIGIOUS ACTION.—Surely, the implied argument continues, surely you are human enough to realise this ? You must see that My conduct is just as natural ; these folk belong to God and I am trying to bring them back to Him. But it looks as if you will not transfer human sentiment to the sphere of religion. You are the friends of God, are you ? It does not seem like it ! Here is the *reproof* of the stories, men losing in Religious Formalism the power of simple universal truths. " With arid heart they blame the Fount of Mercy."

You see no signs in such people that they belong to God ? They are not worth the search ? Well ; the worth of a thing is not altogether in itself but in the opinion of the owner, and God does not hold these folk so cheaply. *All* human souls are precious in His sight ; *He* thinks much of them. To Him they are neither " common nor unclean."

These homely and natural illustrations of our Lord do four things.

1. They explain, justify and *defend* His conduct as the most natural thing possible.

2. They implicitly *reprove* His critics as unsym-

pathetic and unneighbourly—shall we say, inhuman ? ;
at least, out of touch with the Divine mind and will.
They regard themselves as the chosen of God, while
they are really opposed to Him ; they differ from
the standards of Heaven, and its music is to them a
discord. They do not understand the Heart of God.
This is made still clearer in the incident of the Elder
Brother.

3. They *reveal* something of one of the most
splendid facts of Religion—the Craving, Loving,
Shepherding, Following Heart of God. He never
ceases to long for and search for the lost ; He goes on
" until he find it." (These pregnant words are in
both stories.) That means He goes anywhere, everywhere ; it is the Love which finds its climax in Calvary.
He saves " to the uttermost."

The joy at a soul restored can be measured by the
thoroughness of the search, a joy which is felt throughout the courts of Heaven. There is no rivalry or
jealousy there as to who receive the Divine Love ;
in the exquisite words of S. Bernard : " The tears
of the penitent are angels' wine." The more who
share His Love the greater is the joy of each. It is
the joy of a vacant place filled, a longing satisfied.
The soul restored is worth no more than those already
there, but the *joy* of the *return* is more than the joy
of possession : the love to all is the same. Anyone
who has lost and then recovered a single item from a
collection knows this feeling : greater joy over the
one found than over those already there. It is the
inspiration of missionary work.

4. They *declare* the equal value of all men in the
Divine sight. The sinner and the publican are of as

65   E

much moment to God as the Pharisee—the nine or the ninety and nine—a surprising fact to those who heard the stories, and to all self-satisfied and privileged persons. On seeing a wandering sheep the natural question is : to whom does it belong, where ought it to be, where is its home ? Jesus says these belong to God and their place is with Him.

Each one is worth saving ; God's interest is individual. The return of even one makes music in Heaven. Cold statistics and averages do not apply in the sphere of the affections. When a child dies it is no comfort to tell the sorrowing mother that so many hundreds die every year : it is *her* child she mourns. Too often the missions and philanthropies of men are only aroused by numbers : God misses *one*. " There is no place where earth's sorrows are more felt than up in Heaven."

Note.—The Parable of the Lost Sheep is recorded by S. Matthew in connection with the " little ones " ; that they must not be despised. This is really a special use of the great teaching of the story, and may be very profitably applied to the importance of the Child in, and to, the Church.

THE LOST SON

or,

THE HOME-COMING OF A SOUL.

S. LUKE, xv. 11-32.

IN this third of the Parables which deal with the Joy of Recovering something valued and lost, some latent ideas of the others are brought to prominence.

(1) It is *stronger as a Justification of His Conduct.* The scene is now a Home, and the actors the Members of a Family, more poignant than that of a flock of sheep or a treasure of coins. The scale has been an ascending one, not only in numerical proportion— 1 per cent, 10 per cent, 50 per cent—but in quality : a worldly possession, a personal treasure, a son !

(2) The former two only suggested that the *Pharisees* and other critics of His Ministry were unsympathetic, not acting the part of kindly neighbours and friends, non-sharers in the Divine Joy ; this gives *an actual picture* of their conduct in the incident of *The Elder Brother ;* his sulky, pettish, rude behaviour is a Parable of themselves. Jesus' criticism of His critics has developed and is now direct reproof. They are Bad Brothers and Unworthy Sons.

(3) We learn for the first time something of *the*

Feelings of the Lost. These could only be sympathetic-ally imagined in the sheep and had no existence in the silver.

Further, these Feelings of the Lost Son are given as the active *Cause* of his return. In the others there was only the activity of the searchers. Not that the father's joy is thereby less—rather more, since the *Return is a Voluntary Act*, making it truly morally complete. Nor is the graciousness of the Reception in any way dimmed : has he not been watched for ? Is he not seen while " yet a great way off " ? And is he not welcomed with kisses which stop his lips from full confession ? Not a barred door but open arms, not a servant's menial tasks but a much loved son's honoured place, are his experience ; can a father's heart do more ?

(4) This *" Gospel in the Gospel "* is matchless as literature, and to paraphrase it is only to weaken it, perhaps to spoil it. The picture is finished and per-fect. From the peace and plenty of Home to the Husks of the unclean beasts, from self-discovery to the discovery of his father, the scenes follow with a vividness which startle one.

(5) Are we to regard this story as a *transcript of Jewish Life* like the others ? There is nothing to suggest that we must not : rather the other way, since it is the naturalness of the stories that is the ground of His argument. Yet such a picture shames even Christendom ! How many fathers, *even with this Parable before them*, will welcome lost sons like this : meeting them with music and feasts ? Is not the modern father mirrored rather in The Elder Brother ?

There are certain *implications* in the Parable which seem worthy of emphasis.

(1) This is the Parable of the *Freedom of Man*: even God waits till man is willing. No resistance is made to the younger son getting his portion and leaving home; we are sons, not slaves. Only when *he* says, " I will arise," does the Second Act begin. Men are not picked up like coins or sheep; they must " come to themselves," and then come *of* themselves. There are no messages or communications in the story, unless those of memory and prayer, and there must be the consciousness of need and the craving for Home before the face is turned there. It is the Parable of the Human Will: its selfishness, its dangers and its triumphal abasements.

(2) The Thesis of these Parables is that *Heaven is not happy so long as there is a vacant place,* and that the eyes of God are ever towards the return of the wayward. Men shall set no limits to the Father's Heart and Hope; to limit love and forgiveness is to play the Elder Brother. There is not one word of condemnation when the Lost returns; who could upbraid those rags and penitential tears? The returned son understands his Father as he never did before, and his love and service come from the very depths of his willing soul.

(3) *The Perfect Satisfaction of man* is in the Presence and Service of the *Father.* Heaven *is* our Home, and we are akin to God. Living in the material and " seeing life " is to be " dead " : to live with and to serve God is the life and peace of the soul. The motives which turned his face toward Home were not the highest, yet he knows that in this unfeeling and dis-

appointing world the only chance of food and shelter is with his father. The eternal spiritual satisfaction of man is only found in God. The pessimist may say there is nothing good for man ; the secularist may say the things of the world are good enough ; but the hungry soul craves for what is finer and more spiritual. In the factory we are " hands," in the world we are only names, but with God we are *sons*.

(4) *The crisis of the story* for the inmates of the home is the hour of *Reception ;* it is the manner of welcome that divides the characters. In the original intention the Lost Son is a minor character, but his return *tests* the others. The father is whole-hearted in his joy ; the servants share in it also ; but the *brother fails*. It is actually with the one nearest him that there is disappointment. His father may say with gentle reproach, " Thy brother is come," but he has nothing but coarse charges to make, lifting the veil of these past months, and the rude insinuation," this *thy son.*" Thus he separates himself from his brother, and even implies reproof of his father. Here the Pharisees may see their conduct : this is how they act. They would shut the door upon those whom God wants.

A generation later we find the same in the refusal of the Jewish Christians that the Gospel be preached to the Gentiles ; it is the same spirit to-day that decries Evangelism and Foreign Missions ; and many a Christian becomes an Elder Brother when he hears the words " Jewish Missions " ! Let us see to it that we shut the door on no one the Father is longing for.

(5) *What is a Lost Son ?* Where is the Far Country ?

He is a man who has turned his back upon God to live by his own will and pleasure, and the Far Country is simply estrangement from God, the Father. There may be fine clothes upon the back and money in the purse while the spirit goes in rags and hunger and shame. Sons may be lost to God with their names on the rolls of the Churches, and some may be rejoicing in fellowship with Him in unlikely and unorthodox places. God wants all : He wants you.

Someone has said that up to the age of forty a man says to the world, " Give," and then he comes to himself and begins to say, " Forgive " ; but surely it is best of all from the beginning of life to love and serve our Father and our God.

Note.—It is too long for quotation here, but interest and profit may be found in the description of a picture of the Prodigal, given by Thackeray in his Criticial Reviews under the heading " Strictures on Pictures." Cf. Vol. 13, p. 268 (Biographical Edition).

THE UNFAITHFUL HUSBANDMEN

or,

THE FORFEITED PRIVILEGES OF THE JEWISH NATION.

S. MATTHEW, xxi. 33-46. S. MARK, xii. 1-12. S. LUKE, xx. 9-19.

ON previous occasions our Lord had used Parables to defend His Ministry—*e.g.*, The Doctor's Place and The Joy of Finding Lost Property. They had also suggested a criticism of His critics, the last of them in the figure of The Elder Brother holding the mirror up to the Pharisees very plainly. This Parable carries His reproof still further, as *criticism of the Jews* is its *main theme.* Here His criticism becomes condemnation, and at the same time the claim for His own authority is asserted to be the highest possible. He, Who in the early days of His Ministry had been the target for their shafts of amusement and sarcasm, has now become their Judge ; by their conduct towards Him shall they stand or fall in the sight of God. The criticised Friend of the outcast now casts them out.

The locus of the incident gives it a dramatic setting : it is in Jerusalem and in the Temple itself—the very heart of Jewish Religion and Nationality—that He,

Who knows His Cross is near, speaks their doom.
The chief priests and the elders question Him as to
His authority for His words and for such actions as
the Cleansing of the Temple Courts, and He replies
with a counter-question as to the source of the Baptist's authority : have they ever made up their minds
as to that ? Here He has them in a cleft stick : if
they allow that John had Divine Authority (as the
crowd believed), why, then, had they not believed
him ; if his authority was only human they dared not
say so openly to the people. So they answer that they
do not know, and thereby confess their unfitness to
appreciate the authority of Jesus. He refuses, therefore, an answer to their question. Almost immediately
afterwards He turns to the people and speaks this
Parable which contains a fully sufficient answer, as
they are quick enough to perceive.

(1) THE STORY is rather an improbable one ; its
actual occurrence is most unlikely. But this serves
only to emphasise the greatness of the sin to which it
serves as index or parallel ; that men to whom God
had given a serious charge should ignore and then
defy Him is almost unbelievable.

A carefully prepared and fully equipped vineyard
is entrusted to a number of cultivators by a land-
owner who goes abroad. All has been done to make
the vineyard a sure source of profit. At the proper
season he sends a servant to collect his share of the
proceeds, but they maltreat him and send him away
with nothing. Even worse happens to others who
are sent, beating, insulting, wounding and actually
death. Finally he sends his son : his perfect repre-

73

sentative with full authority which they are sure to acknowledge. Instead of that these evil men see now their last and best chance ! If they can dispose of the son they may take the ground into their own hands and keep it permanently ; the owner seems determined not to return. So they murder him. What now, says Jesus, do you think will happen in such a case ? There is but one possible answer : when the owner does come he will punish these men with death, and hand their task over to others who will be faithful.

(2) THE APPLICATION.—The use of The Vine as the symbol of the Jewish people is a familiar one in the Old Testament (Cf. Isaiah, v. 1-7 ; Jeremiah, ii. 21 ; Psalm, lxxx. 8-16). With it go the thoughts of Divine care for it, and Divine hope of fruit from it. Have we here, then, the Vineyard as the emblem of the people, and their Leaders—the Rabbis, Elders and Teachers—represented by the wicked culti- vators ? If that be so, the servants sent by the owner for fruit are the prophets and others (like the Baptist) who came and suffered all kinds of abuse and mal- treatment. This will leave the common people as guiltless as the innocent vines. In the record, how- ever, we find the *nation* held as *guilty :* " The kingdom of God shall be taken away from you, and shall be given to a nation bringing forth the fruits thereof " (S. Matthew, xxi. 43).

On the whole it seems better not to distinguish between the people and their leaders, but to regard the whole nation as one in their trust given them by God. As the owner gave to certain men the charge of his carefully prepared vineyard, so God gave to His elect and chosen people the knowledge of His Will, and lavished upon them all that care and love could do to make them fruitful in good works. This trust of the Divine Law they held for the good of the world and the glory of God, but they have been faithless to their charge and have *kept it to themselves*. Great prophetic men whom God sent to recall the nation to the true understanding of the Divine Purpose were unheeded, were abused and even killed. The Jews were proud that they were the chosen and privileged of God, but they neglected the duty which such privileges entailed. They served themselves, not the Will of God. People and teachers are alike guilty. The fate of the latest and last messenger of the owner has not yet been paralleled in their history, but the implication is there that this *last appeal is being made in the person of the Speaker*. Jesus knows the murderous feelings of their hearts ; and we know that very soon, not the rulers only but the populace (doubtless at their instigation) joined in the shouts to Pilate, " Crucify Him ! Crucify HIM ! "

When the priests and elders hear the Master answer His own question as to the proper punishment of these faithless and murderous husbandmen, they say, " God forbid ! " But Jesus quotes against them a passage from the Psalms (cxviii. 22, 23) as to the rejected stone, *i.e.*, Himself, becoming the chief cornerstone, which will decide man's destiny, and then foretells the certain transference of privilege and duty.

TWO LESSONS seem clear in this Parable and its attendant incidents.

(1) There is an *Exposure of the Dangers of Privilege*. So thorough has been the revolt of the Jews against the Divine authority that they do not recognise His latest Messenger as from God at all : " the most complete and authentic of all." In their rejection of The Son " there is a telling representation of the fact of the decay in Jesus' time of the sense of the nearness and reality of God " (Menzies). If they ever thought of Him they thought of Him as far away ; He was only in the background of their thoughts. Now Privilege means either Performance or Punishment ; God does not leave His work for ever undone ; and a trust undischarged is handed over to others. Nations cannot live on names and tradition ; unless they serve as they are meant to, and are able to, they will be removed to make way for honester men. It is easy to forget duty and to rest on privilege, but *God's elections are all for usefulness :* a nation to serve other nations, a man and a ministry to serve and bless other men. It is not enough to know the Gospel ; it must be made known ; it is a grave matter to be in the Christian Ministry, for without the good of men and the glory of God ever directing and inspiring, it is neither a ministry nor is it Christian. As the servant must ever be mindful of his lord's honour and profit, so the profit of God is the good of the souls of men. The danger of a professional priesthood is that it lives for itself ; a true ministry is for the well-being of the kingdom and the honour of the King.

(2) There is here *a Revelation of Jesus*. In speaking of His own death and its consequences, how by killing Him they would not be done with Him but rather bring their national career to a suicidal climax, the

Parable passes into Prophecy. "The story describes the history of Israel, and implies that Jesus felt Himself to be God's last appeal to His people, and also thought their rejection of Him would issue in His becoming the foundation of a new community which should inherit God's Kingdom" (Peake).

He is the final appeal of God to men, and His servants must ever seek to make mankind realise that in Him we have the Incarnate Will and Word and Way of His Father. *He* knew the meaning of Authority and Obedience if these men did not—an Obedience which meant going consciously to death. He never forgot God : His meat was to do the Father's will and to finish His work, even though "It is finished!" had to be spoken on the Cross. His followers must be ready, too, to take up the Cross, if God so wills it.

THE LABOURERS IN THE VINEYARD

or,

THE SURPRISING GRACE OF GOD.

S. MATTHEW, xix. 30—xx. 16.

THE OCCASION.—A rich young man had been unable to make the sacrifice Jesus called for (xix. 16-22). Peter and the other disciples consider that *they* have made sacrifices for Jesus, and he inquires of the Master if this will not be rewarded in some fashion (xix. 27). The answer is that both they and all others who have made sacrifices for Him will be recompensed, not only justly, but most generously (xix. 28, 29). " But the *spirit* of Peter's question required an answer too." It savoured rather much of the market-place and of bargaining ; there was selfish expectancy in it ; and so there follows a warning. Sacrifice will not go unrewarded, " but "—and here one almost sees the arresting hand and warning finger—human expectancies may be reversed with God ; there are surprises waiting on the other side ; God's settlements at the end of the day will show strange reversals ; " but many that are first shall be last ; and the last first " (xix. 30). And then He tells this story of a vinegrower who did many unexpected things, as a warning against the introduction of the mercenary spirit into the Realm of Grace. It is not a picture of the future : it is no more than a caution against low motive in Christ's service. " Respectu apostolorum non est praedictio, sed admonitio."

THE STORY.—The centre of gravity here is not in the workers, but in the farmer : " The kingdom of heaven is like unto a *man* that is an householder, &c." The Kingdom will be as full of surprises as this man's conduct.

(1) He keeps hiring workers all day long, from early morning till within an hour of closing time. Employers do not behave like that either in the East or in the West, but it looks as if this man cannot bear to see idle men ; he pities their condition and contrives to find occupation for them even at the eleventh hour. This is at least unusual : may we not call it even eccentrically kind ?

(2) When the time comes for payment he bids his steward call the last-hired to come first. This must not be pressed as if here we had the " last " becoming " first " : that would be a bald literalism foreign to the story ; but, as Dr Bruce points out, it is at least an index to the farmer's mind : he has these unfortunate fellows much in his thoughts, and has a special interest in them. That the last-hired should be the first paid is another unusual act, and it draws the attention of the others at once. What he intends doing has to be done in the presence of the others, or it loses all point.

(3) He pays these workers a full day's wage. This

is the most surprising thing of all, quite unexpected by the recipients and unlooked for by everybody else ; but it enables these men to go home with a light heart to wife and family. Work had been given them, and now bounty is added. The employer finds his pleasure in their surprised delight. To make a practice of this would soon ruin an ordinary employer, for he would find workers scarce in the morning but easily found in the afternoon, if they knew that labour for half a day or for even a single hour would bring full wages. But this farmer is not an ordinary one, he is quite an unusual and exceptional person, more intent upon helping folk than making grapes pay. He has more delight and satisfaction in men than in grapes.

(4) These three actions show a kindly, gracious and individual generosity. When we seek for a reason we find none but his own pleasure. It is his nature to do such things, kindly things not to be measured by the ordinary canons of business. But that Justice is not forgotten is shown by the next surprising act in the story : those who have worked the whole day got their promised wages, but that only. In view of what has happened this may seem Justice strict to the point of severity. The criticism is natural, but does not look deep enough into the hearts of the crowd.

Observe that generosity to some did not exceed justice to others, and that what both received was the day's wages necessary for life and home. When they who had borne the burden and heat of the day saw the latecomers so surprised and delighted with their entirely unexpected reward, they seem to have *expected more than they had earned.* The eleventh-hour men looked for a trifle and unexpectedly received a sufficiency ; payment far in excess of their conscious deserts : the others seem to look for more than a sufficiency—*i.e.*, for more than their deserts. They certainly did begrudge their fellows getting as much as they did. Theirs is a mercenary, grudging and unneighbourly spirit, resentful of a kindness to others ; and they murmur at their employer as if he had done them a wrong, as if benevolence to one spells injustice to another, and as if the extra pay were coming out of their pockets ! They do not seem in the least pleased and sympathetic that these men of their own class, so unfortunate in the matter of work, should at the end of the day receive a day's wage, but rather find in it a cause for grumbling and grudging. It is the Prodigal's brother over again.

To the ringleader among his critics the farmer sharply says : " Friend, I do thee no wrong ; didst thou not agree with me for a penny ? " Does my *kindness* justify your *grudge ?* Are you envious because I am liberal ? Have you not received what you earned ? To complain that others receive rather more than they earned marks you as selfish and narrow. The others do get more than they earned—some of them ten times more—and the reason of their getting lies in my own goodwill ; it has nothing to do with desert, only with grace. Why be ungracious because I am gracious ?

Yet he does not throw money away ; all get a sufficiency, none a superfluity. It has been argued that since all received a penny, therefore all received alike. That is true in word but not in spirit, and the late-

comers appreciate the generosity of their treatment :
the last are first, and the first last.

LESSON.—God's Kingdom is a Kingdom of Grace,
and the acts of grace are startling and unwelcome to
the bargaining and narrow spirit. At the end of the
day, when God settles with His servants, those whose
chances of service were few or late will be amazed
at the exceeding goodness of God, for they find Him
not only " just " (v. 4) but also " gracious " (v. 15).
God loves to give every man a chance and a blessing.
Peter and his companions may justly look forward
to reward " when the Son of man shall sit in the
throne of His glory " (xix. 28), but there will be surprises also when some we never considered real workers
for God will win the welcome and sunshine of the
Father's face—surprises both to them and to others.

This is entirely of a piece with the whole Teaching
of our Lord regarding the Nature of God. The Lost
Son has a slight hope that he may become equal with
the hired servants of his father ; to his amazement
he finds himself an honoured guest and a son beloved,
while the elder brother stands amazed and aggrieved
at the whole proceeding. The woman with the
alabaster box of precious perfume crouches at the
Master's feet, striving dumbly to express her soul :
she goes from the Presence with the glory of forgiveness ringing in her ears and heart, while Simon sits
silent, reproved and wondering. The Penitent Thief
prays for remembrance by Christ in His Kingdom
one day : he is promised Christ's companionship that
very day in Paradise ! The last shall be first : God's
Kingdom is of Grace, not of Wages : " the *gift* of

God is eternal life " ; God is ever forgiving. It was the Magdalene who first saw the Risen Lord. There are " out-castes " and " niggers " and " natives " in India, Africa and America to-day whose welcome by their Saviour will be one of the surprises at the end of the day.

To serve God for any other reason than that it is God we serve is to choose the low instead of the high. " Doth Job serve God for naught ? " is the sneering question of the devil. Love makes no calculations, and true Christian Devotion seeks but to please God, without thought of self or hope or glory.

IV.

THE
CITIZENSHIP OF THE KINGDOM.

THE PHARISEE AND THE PUBLICAN

or,

OF WHOM DOES GOD APPROVE?

S. LUKE, xviii. 9-14.

THIS is not strictly a Parable—*i.e.*, it is not an incident taken from Human Life or Nature to suggest or illustrate spiritual truths. It is an illustration taken from the sphere itself to which the moral belongs. It is an example, not a parallel; a photograph, not a mirror. The characters are ourselves.

It was spoken directly to those who seemed to require its warning—certain self-righteous and censorious persons, but it carries also its message of hope to the penitent.

Every word of the story repays study; it is rich in detail—*e.g.*, when the Pharisee says, " even as this publican," is he not finding matter for self-complacency in the retired position, the penitent acts and attitude of the other, so unlike what he feels himself entitled to? One can almost see the contemptuous pointed finger.

THE LIKENESSES BETWEEN THE TWO.—In some ways they are much alike.

(1) *Both men go up to the Temple to pray.* Time and again in His Teaching our Lord just assumes the habit of Prayer, although He has much to say as to its spirit and manner. He was ever a Man of Prayer Himself. Further, is there a more fitting place for the penitent sinner than the House of God ? The Church is not for the righteous alone, but for every sinner seeking God.

(2) *Both are intensely personal.* The Pharisee uses the first person five times in twenty-nine words in the Greek—in English it is five in thirty-four—and the average of the other is much the same : one in six ; in English, one in seven. It is by their prayers that they are judged, for if ever a man is sincere it is when his thoughts and words are known to God alone. Nothing is so self-revealing as Prayer. Bengel says : " In precibus totus status animae exercetur " ; and here, indeed, we read the minds of two men.

(3) *What they say about themselves is undoubtedly true.* Whatever were the actual faults of the publican they were unquestionably sinful enough ; and the virtues of the Pharisee are quite positive things : he *was* a just, honourable and moral man, religious, self-respecting and abstemious. The *question* is not as to the facts, but as to *their attitude to the facts :* do the virtues of the one justify self-complacency before God, and the sin of the other take away all hope ?

THE DIFFERENCES BETWEEN THEM.—This is the important matter.

(1) The standard of the Pharisee is that of *Conduct* alone. He judges himself and others by the external, by action, by morality. He limits his vision to man,

and sees no higher than earth. He is full of what *he* has done or avoided, and so becomes critical and censorious about those who do less or are less careful. There is a touch of The Elder Brother in the way he speaks. " The vulgar method of self-exaltation by depreciation of others has been and is too commonly practised."

(2) The standard of the Publican is that of *Feeling*. He judges himself by his relationship to God, and to God only. There is a sense in which we may say that he resembles the Pharisee in having other men in his view, when he calls himself " the sinner " ; but it is a comparison which puts him at the bottom, not the top. It is the attitude of one who, when first convinced of sin, thinks no other man's sins can equal his own. There is an echo of The Lost and Returning Son here.

The difference between the two is the difference between fulfilling the code of outward morality and being consciously a child of God. The one reaches a state of spiritual contentment, while the other is ever seeking to know more of God's will and to come nearer to His heart. The one is fixed, finished, immobile ; the other has constant aspiration and is never content : he can only be at rest in God. His is the humility which sees the Holiness of God, and from the very ground—from the " fearful pit " itself —is drawn to the Father. He who knows his need will be satisfied, not with himself but with the Highest only. The true beginning of the religious life is the hunger and thirst after righteousness : it is the hunger of the Prodigal. " Blessed are the poor in spirit : for theirs is the kingdom of heaven."

" The church is the one institution in the modern world whose sole business is to create in men dissatisfaction with their own characters, their achievements and ideals. . . . This ceaseless insistence that humanity is capable of better things ; this unrelenting challenge to higher thinking, nobler action, more unselfish living—this makes the church a great constructive power." (Cf. " What can a man believe ? " ; by Bruce Barton, p. 57.)

(3) *The Publican does not specify either the Nature or the Amount of his Sin ;* he calls himself plainly " the sinner." In his work as a Tax-gatherer for the Roman overlord he had many opportunities for trickery and extortion, but it is not what he has done or has neglected to do that is the cause of his misery : it is that he feels himself out of touch with God, and his heart is driven by fierce and foul emotions. This is fortunate for us : had his wrong been specified then one whose evil life was quite different might have looked here in vain for hope, but " the sinner " covers us all, and in the Publican we each find ourselves. Estrangement from God by sin is common to all penitent souls.

(4) A very important *distinction* exists between them, in that the one is thinking of " *sins* " and the other of " *sin.*" There is a difference here which separates whole theologies and divides Christendom. To deal with confession of separate acts of sin, with penance, merit and so on, is very different from seeking to make a soul right with God in its constant temper and desire. A personal conviction of sin leads to the Publican's prayer, and to his blessing. Life is a unit, which must be set right with God from the

centre, not the circumference : the sense of sin begins the making of saints. Read religious autobiographies.

There is a principle applying here in all spheres. The man who dwells complacently on what he has done—the books written, the pictures painted, the business created, the money saved, the congregation organised—may be in many ways quite excellent, but the secret of greatness is no longer in him. He knows nothing of a discontent which prompts to higher things, nothing of the artist soul whose *next* effort is ever the best, which forgets the things behind and reaches forward. He has ceased to grow—*i.e.*, to live.

(5) The Pharisee is *satisfied with himself*, and has nothing more to hope for ; the Publican has *hope only in the Mercy of God*. An American Divine has said that the Publican's Prayer is Calvinism, and certainly it is the essence of Evangelical Christianity. Man has nothing in or of himself to plead, and casts himself upon the Grace of God.

But let a man beware of thinking too lightly of the Divine Love, of regarding The Father as easy and indulgent. It is not such a conception that makes a man beat his breast. That is why Ruskin speaks of this " delicious parable, savouriest of all Scripture to rogues." It is because of the high and holy nature of the Father's Love that Sin is so exceedingly sinful ; and His Love to His children and His hatred of Sin are found in the Cross. That is the measure of Sin and the promise of Mercy.

(6) How far the Publican was *conscious* of being " justified " in God's sight is difficult to say ; he may have gone away in deepened gloom, and the other

more self-confident than before. But in the sight of God the two men are valued very differently ; the scales of heaven reverse their judgments ; and every penitent to whom this story comes may hold this humble hope of acceptance with Him. The one has the frown, the other the favour, of Heaven. " The bruised reed He will not break, the smoking flax He will not quench " ; " for everyone that exalteth himself shall be humbled : but he that humbleth himself shall be exalted." " It is a universal law of the moral world, true both of God and man, that self-exaltation provokes in others condemnation, and self-humiliation gentle judgment " (Bruce).

Note.—This quotation from ' The Upton Letters ' (Benson), page 20, has a very modern message. " Nowadays the Parable of the Pharisee and the publican is reversed. The Pharisee tells his friends that he is in reality far worse than the publican, while the publican thanks God that he is not a Pharisee. It is only, after all, a different kind of affectation, and perhaps more dangerous, because it passes under the disguise of a virtue. We are all miserable sinners, of course, but it is no encouragement to goodness if we try to reduce ourselves all to the same level of conscious corruption. The only advantage would be if, by our humility, we avoided censoriousness."

THE GOOD SAMARITAN

or,

WHAT A "NEIGHBOUR" MEANS.

S. LUKE, x. 25-37.

THIS is the first of several stories given by S. Luke which are not strictly Parables—*i.e.*, they *teach by example* rather than by symbol. They are not taken from another sphere to illustrate by analogy, but belong to the very region of the desired moral. They are imaginary as a stage-play is, yet referring to possible acts. It is very dramatic.

THE OCCASION.—(1) It has its occasion in a question by a lawyer or jurist as to conduct which would lead to eternal life. Jesus refers him to the Law and asks what he finds there. The answer to this is very fine, combining Religion and Morality—God and one's neighbour—in words which entirely satisfy the Master. This combination is now a commonplace of Christian Teaching if not Practice, but from the lips of a lawyer of the period is unexpectedly splendid.

(2) But what does the word "neighbour" cover, he will further learn; how is one to recognise such; what are the limits of neighbourhood and of love;

" who *is* my neighbour ? " It seems an honest attempt to ascertain the limits of responsibility, to scan the sphere of personal duty, as he takes for granted that *not all* are neighbours : some are surely excluded. Now, there are some questions best answered by asking another ; and this Jesus proceeds to do, prefacing His question by telling this story. The definition of " who " his neighbour is means limitation ; the mention of race or class implies the exclusion of others : so the Master seeks to correct his assumption as to limitation by showing *what* a neighbour is. He captures the sympathies with a simple story, and then gently pushes the lesson home by making the lawyer apply it.

The answer is thus indirect but radical, going down to the very first principles of humanity. A child can read, enjoy and profit by the story, yet it is as profound as the essential truth of human relationships. It is a treatise on practical ethics which cannot be improved.

THE STORY.—(1) Of the *sufferer* in the tale we are told nothing at all ; he is just " a man," " somebody," " a human being," and is thus co-extensive with humanity. The others are mentioned in such a way as to suggest certain expectations from them : " a priest," " a Levite," men in the service of God, from whom one might expect something good ; " a Samaritan," one who on Jewish soil would probably be very self-contained and indifferent about others. But the only appeal of the wounded man for pity and care is simply his *humanity ;* he is a distressed and broken man, that is all.

The road from Jerusalem to Jericho is twenty-one miles long and falls over 3,700 feet ; it has always had a bad name—part of it used to be called " The Bloody Way "—and here, as recently as 1820, Sir Frederick Henniker was murdered by Arab robbers. Here the unknown is beset by men who rob him, strip him and treat him so savagely that unless there come speedy help, death is certain ere night falls.

(2) That three men should appear there in a short space of time is quite unlikely, but for the sake of the story the Teller asks us to allow the " coincidence " or " chance." Possibly all were mounted ; the third certainly was, for he is very far from home. The first two are connected with the National Worship ; but both, although seeing the sufferer lying in his blood, *do nothing ;* and that is where they fail. They are quite moral men who would never dream of attacking or robbing another, yet they are inhuman. To be sure they had many excellently sounding reasons to give for this :—clearly there are evil men about ; it will be my turn next ; I cannot stay ; perhaps this is one of the evil band itself ; he seems too far gone for help now, I can do nothing ; and in any case I am not a doctor ; if someone comes and sees me stooping over him they will think it is my doing and that I am robbing him ; there are important duties awaiting the priest at Jericho, or his family is already expecting him, and relief will come better from that Levite behind him ; the priest has done nothing, says the Levite, and I shall follow my superior's example ; there is nothing left to show if he be Jew or Gentile, and I cannot afford either the time, trouble or expense

95

of assisting him. Excuses for inaction sometimes take
high-sounding names :

> " Because I held upon my selfish road,
>   And left a brother wounded by the way,
>   And called ambition, duty, and pressed on——
>   O Lord, I do repent."

So, with pity for his distress and regret for their
own inability to assist, they pace on, and the sufferer,
with added anguish and despair, hears their steps
die away in the distance. There can be no excuse
for such inaction.

(3) But—and here the listeners feel there is a
change coming—a third traveller, mounted and
carrying such things as a traveller might require on
a long journey from home, comes up, and halts in
pity. Samaritan though he is, he is a *man*—a man
with a heart, and a head and a hand, as he soon
shows. He is a most active and practical person ;
we see this in the immediate help he gives, and in the
arrangements made at the inn alike for the present and
the future. He stresses the first person in speaking
to the inn-keeper, as if he were well known to him,
and then goes about his own affairs contentedly,
with a lighter heart and a lighter purse ! In all this
he overcame the risk of *danger* to himself, his *prejudices*
of Race and Religion, the *delay* in his private affairs,
and the natural *disinclination* of anyone to expend
sympathy, time, trouble and money on a stranger.
He seems, indeed, to have thought of nothing but the
stranger from the time he found him.

The sight of misery and distress moves people in
general ; but some it moves to such action as will

remove the trouble, and others only to remove themselves from the neighbourhood that they may no more be tried. Emotion, without action, is a kind of selfishness ; there is a luxury of tears, and feeling may debauch the soul. Unless the waters of the rising well overflow in streams that refresh they sink back into stagnation and foulness. One may suffer from an overdose of sentiment.

> " Prune thou thy words, thy thoughts control,
>   That o'er thee swell and throng,
> They will condense within thy soul
>   And change to purpose strong.
> But he who lets his feelings run
>   In soft lascivious flow,
> Shrinks where hard service must be done
>   And faints at every blow.
> Faith's meanest deed more favour bears
>   Where hearts and wills are weighed,
> Than brightest transports, choicest prayers,
>   Which bloom their hour and fade."

Even Charity may be selfish, and the coin to the beggar no more than a sop to conscience to prevent one from facing up to the fulness of humanity. This man was *thorough* in his kindness, and did not cease until he saw the sufferer on the sure road to health. To find the beggar a job of work is much more trouble, but it is thorough. The sores and discontents among us will not yield to doles, and sentiments and prayers, but to hard thinking, thorough study and personal effort. Men hate those they injure, they dislike those they neglect, but they love those they have helped. The Samaritan's service was a *personal* one ; he helped neither by proxy nor by officials ; we shall ever best alleviate what we consent to share. Cf. The Epistle of S. James, ii. 14-17.

THE APPLICATION.—The story told, there comes the question : " Which of these three men, in your opinion, proved a neighbour to the man who fell among the robbers ? " Whether the lawyer is so deeply impressed by the Samaritan's action as to forget that he was a Samaritan, and centres upon the acts of his pity, or whether he refuses even now to utter the hated name, we cannot say ; but he replies : " The man who took pity on him." " Then," says Jesus, " go and do the same." Wherever you can show pity, there is your neighbour !

The lawyer has asked *who* was his neighbour : he has learned *what* it is to be one. To be a neighbour is to know nothing of race, rank, or religion—colour, caste, or creed—but to feel and to show *humanity*. The only limitation of neighbourhood is the need of man, and our responsibility comes with our opportunity. Our limits are our powers ; what we can do is ours to do ; our responsibility is our ability to respond. Real Charity is true Sanctity. The lawyer wished Jesus to draw a circle—a wide one, certainly, but still a circle bounding life and service : Jesus takes him to the centre, and from it makes him look out on mankind. He has commended the action of the Samaritan : surely a Jew can do no less !

Where we are is *our* neighbourhood, and those we meet are *our* neighbours. The man you can be neighbourly to, is your neighbour.

THE RICH FOOL

or,

LIFE *VERSUS* POSSESSIONS.

S. LUKE, xii. 15-21.

S. LUKE is the only evangelist who records this story and the incident which promoted it. It is an illustration and example of the truth it teaches rather than a Parable.

THE OCCASION.—An unusually large crowd has assembled round the famous Teacher, and all are listening to the advice and warnings He gives His disciples. This includes a reference (v. 11) to the magistrates and courts of the country ; and one of the crowd—a man with a grievance against his brother as to the division of property—breaks in at this point and asks Him to speak to the offender to give him his proper share. That such a request was made says much for the place Jesus held in public repute ; yet the interrupter is so full of his own trouble that he does not take in the greatness of the words he has just heard as to trust in God for this world and the next (vv. 4-7) ; he cannot see past the immediate need he himself has. He is not the only one who comes into the Saviour's Presence with worldly burdens pressing

99

so close that higher things are obscured. A man may take the world with him into Church, and miss God by the Material crowding out the Spiritual. The tumult of one's own feelings prevents the hearing of the still, small Voice.

It is quite possible that he was suffering from an act of real injustice, and that his case against the offending brother was a good one, but our Lord refuses to enter into its consideration. He does not find Himself called upon to act as arbiter in such matters. Certainly He came to serve men ; but in the things of the spirit, not the purse. The Church shall give men the vision of God, and of their neighbour in sympathy and justice, but it shall not judge in details of wealth and wages. It seeks to reach the heart and touch the springs of conduct. This man's hot heart gets a chilling word (v. 14), and then Jesus turns to the crowd and gives a general warning against longing for money : " See and keep clear of covetousness in every shape and form." Even in an affair of justice the craving for money may be latent ; and, no matter how much a man may possess, his possessions are really no part of his true life. Life is no part of one's possessions. Then follows His story to give point to this.

THE STORY.—A well-to-do farmer has such a fine harvest that he has to do something about it, so he reasons the matter out, and decides on building larger granaries to hold his stuff. At the same time he makes up his mind to retire from active work when this has been done, since he now has ample stores for years to come, and he looks forward to finding satisfaction and enjoyment in their use and consumption. The best thing he sees for his " soul " is a long rest, with plenty to eat and drink, and a good time generally. There is nothing evil, nothing debauched and gross, in his programme : *nothing but himself*. He makes his wealth his master, not his servant, and hangs his happiness upon it ! Are not his time, his life and his money his own ?

On the very night of this satisfactory conclusion, however, another call comes of a very different kind. God speaks to him and calls him " foolish," tells him that the soul to which he had promised such comfort is wanted where these things cannot come, and asks him who will then enjoy all his stores. (This midnight voice of God may well be the man's own reflections, when he feels himself struck by some sudden and mortal illness.) Such, adds Jesus, is the fate of men who care only for the wealth of earth and never think of God. Their souls have no comfort now, for they are penniless in the currency of Heaven ; all that gave them comfort is gone. If to enjoy such things is one's highest joy, one's life, one's Heaven, what will it be to lose them ?

THE APPLICATION.—(1) *Our Attitude to Money is a Spiritual Test*. Neither Privations nor Possessions should affect one's faith in God. There is such a thing as Mastery by the Material, and such a mastery will endanger and may ruin the soul. The amassing of wealth may be most innocent—nay ! a splendid game or conflict—and yet the possession may be a spiritual danger : *money is not a value in Life*. This man's wealth was honestly and diligently acquired, yet it led him to forget or neglect God : the gift obscured the Giver. His vision becomes bounded by his barns. He becomes entirely self-centred : notice the frequency of the first personal pronoun in his words. He gives no thought to the homes of the widow and orphan which might have been made the barns of his superfluity. What the " ground " brought forth and gave him, he calls " *my* " crops.

New circumstances always call for fresh adjustments ; this man adjusted his soul to his circumstances. Prosperity induced worldliness, and he sank himself in the abundance of his possessions. " If riches increase, set not thine heart upon them." There is more danger of being spiritually choked by prosperity than by poverty. Increasing riches tend to starve the soul by increasing the selfish propensities which are latent in it. This is part of the " deceitfulness " of riches. A full cup is ill to carry. In the ' Purgatorio,' Dante makes the avaricious say that

> " Avarice had extinguished our affection
> For every good, whereby was action lost " ;

and the cause of this powerlessness and general demoralisation of soul is that such an one becomes " a wretched soul and parted from God." These last words are the secret : that " covetousness which is idolatry " preys upon the soul and draws the interests and affections from God and kindness, towards money and money's enjoyment, and thus gradually *separates man from God*. To have one's affections set on things below and not above finds its penalty, according to Dante, in the doom of ever being turned downwards, prone upon the ground, grasping the mire and choking in the dust :

> " Even as our eye did not uplift itself
> Aloft, being fastened upon earthly things,
> So justice here has merged it in the earth."

Remember the picture also of Mammon in ' Paradise Lost ' :—

> " . . . the least erected spirit that fell
> From heaven ; for e'en in heaven his looks and thoughts
> Were always downwards bent, admiring more
> The riches of heaven's pavement, trodden gold,
> Than aught divine or holy else enjoyed
> In vision beatific."

Well does the aged Apostle write : " My little children, guard yourselves from idols." " Covetousness, which *is* idolatry." Read also the account of The Man with the Muck Rake, which Bunyan's Pilgrim saw in the Interpreter's House.

(2) Less on the surface is the Lesson of *The Uncertainty of Life*. It is unpurchasable. This man was confident of the future, but he never saw those years which he mapped out so delightfully. (Cf. The Epistle of S. James, iv. 13-15.) He may have been a prudent and able man in human judgment ; God terms him " foolish " : he spoke of " many years " ; God recalls him to " this night " : and the pampering which he looked forward to for his " soul " is swept away in " is required of thee." We all hold life on a feeble tenure, and one somewhat advanced in life, as he surely was, should have remembered that the more years one has had there are the fewer to come. Time is but a part of eternity, and Character is being formed

now. What are your Life's ideals; where is your Treasure—and your Heart?

(3) There is here the further truth of *The Reality of God*. Life and Time are not ours to hold, but happy is the man who holds to God. Those who plan the greatness of their Babel have forgotten God, and prove themselves fools. The correct answer to the sum will not come when you drop a figure; and in the sum of Life the chief Figure is God. It is right and necessary to plan one's life, to labour and to care for one's dependants; yet we never know " how it will go with us " (Philippians, ii. 23); that is the condition which should always be understood. Unfortunately this man, like many others, did not remember it.

Our times are in God's hand, and He is a Father Who loves and cares (vv. 6, 7). What is God to you? Is He the Master and Controller; do you find in His Will your Peace—or your Terror? Let us praise the Giver, and not the gifts; let us rest our all upon Him, knowing that He makes no mistakes, only we.

" The supreme need is the freedom of the soul from the bondage of materialism. There can be no earthly paradise for man until he is spiritually minded."

THE IMPORTUNATE WIDOW

or,

THE SUCCESS OF UNSHAKEN FAITH.

S. LUKE, xviii. 1-8.

THE use of unworthy and unlikely characters is not infrequent in Our Lord's Parables. It makes an *a fortiori* argument : when an evil person does a commendable action, how much more certain is it that the good Father will do it ! The firing of a gun near one is startlingly harsh, but the echoes from the distant hills make music : this story is harsh at a first hearing, but when we catch its heavenly echo we find it sweet.

THE CHARACTERS.—(1) *The Judge*. We are in the East ; nearly 2000 years ago. Secure in his position the man cares for nothing but himself. He names the name of God, but has no reverence for Him or His Law : he is without conscience. Public Opinion he laughs at. He is not to be moved by Sanctity or Society ; God and Justice are only words. He is a scoundrel but not a hypocrite, for he acknowledges these things to himself quite readily (v. 4) ; he is just as black as he is painted, and does not care a whit that it is so.

(2) *The Widow.* Throughout Scripture one finds the Widow the constant type of helplessness, the easy prey of injustice and fraud. (Cf. Job, xxix. 13 ; Isaiah, x. 2 ; S. Luke, vii. 12 ; Epistle of James, i. 27 ; &c.). She is alone—worse than alone, for there is one who has done her a wrong ; and she has no plea but Justice. *Her cause is just,* or she would never have appeared and persisted as she does, but what is Justice to such a Judge as this ? Of all persons she is the most unlikely to succeed.

THE STORY.—Besides fair play, which seems hopeless, there are three ways in which one might hope for a favourable verdict from this man. He might be *bribed ;* clearly she cannot do that—probably it is her money she seeks from her opponent. He might be *bullied :* her unsupported womanhood cannot do that. What remains ? Only her tongue : the judge may be *bothered* into doing something for her. So what she can do she does most thoroughly ; she *persists* in her appearing before him, her appeal becoming shriller and shriller as the days pass, until she threatens to become a nuisance. The judge at last takes some notice of her : if this woman is not got rid of, she will be flying at me with her nails some day ! (v. 5).

To attend to her plea at first meant trouble : *not* to attend to it is going to mean greater trouble. The fondness for his own comfort, which was her foe in the beginning, becomes her friend at the finish. He was vulnerable only on the side of his selfishness, and at long last she gets under his guard there. His reason for not listening becomes a reason for listening, and she is sent away one day happy in her success. She had no idea that this day was to be in any way different from those before it : her answer came quite unexpectedly. She knew nothing of what was going on in the judge's mind.

INTERPRETATION.—The Lesson of this rather unpleasing, though not unhumorous, story is that *Persistent Unshaken Faith will meet with Success*, and that very unexpectedly, perhaps, when it comes. Prayer is the voice of Faith, and Persistent Prayer has the certainty of a favourable answer. If this judge, who *was* so unwilling to grant the Widow's request, at last did so, shall not the Judge of all, Who only *seems* unwilling to our hasty and narrow thinking, most assuredly answer the cry of His people ? The worse one thinks of the judge the more encouragement does the story hold for him who believes in God. Dante wrote :—

> " . . . . Fervent love
> And lively hope, with violence assail
> The kingdom of the heavens, and overcome
> The will of the Most High : not in such sort
> As man prevails o'er man ; but conquers it
> Because 'tis willing to be conquered, still,
> Though conquered, by its mercy conquering."

The fact that God seems to be presented here in a very unfriendly guise is felt by some to be a difficulty, but it need not be so. The judge represents God, not as He is in Himself, but as He may sometimes seem to us, unheeding. Delay in answering prayer may appear to our haste and anxiety to be hard, but the lesson is that man must never be induced to think, from any delay whatever, that God does not care. That must never be said. Mysterious delay may be sorely trying, but *Right will be done :* that is never to be in doubt.

Faith in God—a faith which never fails—is the essential of successful prayer. This differs entirely from the " vain repetitions " of the pagan, which have only sound in them without meaning and real desire. *Every time* this widow made her appeal to the judge she *meant each word* she said : she was real, intense, determined. It is thus that men are to pray. Words are nothing : the faith behind the words is power. With that one may confidently assail the walls of heaven !

CONCLUSION.—The Parable concludes with a *Promise* and a *Warning.*

(1) God will see justice done, if men cry unto Him day and night. God is God ; His nature is to be just and to see justice wrought out. Never let men give up hope : the evils of the world are to be cured by God, if men will only pray ! When least they think it, the answer is about to come. God speaks, and it is done. Revival will come, when men *mean* it.

(2) In spite of this promise, however, Jesus says that men will lose heart and hope, so that faith will be hard to find. We shall disappoint God, because we are disappointed in Him so soon. Do we ever feel tempted to despair of God ? Is the Church never losing faith in the certainty of the Master's triumph ? " When the Son of Man cometh " (v. 8) connects this Parable with the previous chapter on The Second

Coming, and thus warns the Church against all care-lessness, hopelessness, despair and prayerlessness. Faith and Prayer are ours—nay! victory is ours, since God will assuredly answer.

Note.—The story of the Syrophenician Mother is an excellent commentary on this Parable. Cf. S. Mark, vii. 24-30.

THE IMPORTUNATE FRIEND

or,

THE SECRET OF SUCCESSFUL PRAYER.

S. LUKE, xi. 5-13.

THE disciples have been taught *what* to pray : they are now to learn *how* to pray. Possession of a weapon is not enough ; there must follow instruction in its use : Saul's sword needs Saul's efficiency. This Parable teaches us at least two great lessons : the Persistent Spirit which alone makes Prayer efficient, and the Certainty of Success as the reason for that Persistence—*i.e.,* how to make Prayer a Success. The need and practice of Prayer are assumed as facts of human experience ; God is not a blind Force but an Understanding Heart which feels with, and answers, man.

THE STORY.—It is very simple, most felicitous, and not without humour. Eastern travellers frequently travelled by night to escape the scorching heat of day, and one unexpectedly arrives at a friend's house late one night. The hour is seasonable for the visitor but unseasonable for the host, as his cupboard is empty, the day's supply of bread being exhausted ; and he hurries to a neighbour's house to procure some. There is no improvidence here ; the call is quite unlooked for, and the duty of hospitality is too sacred to allow any consideration of disturbing his neighbour to stand in the way. He is doing as he would be done by, and he is not begging, he is borrowing. Three of the flat loaves then used will suffice.

Having aroused his neighbour he hails him " friend," and explains the situation, but the response from within lacks the kindly word " friend "—an ominous omission. " Don't bother me," he says, in a tone as crusty as his loaves ; there's not much " friendship " in disturbing one at midnight ! Then follows a string of reasons, or rather excuses, for his churlish rejoinder. The one entirely valid reason for refusal—an empty cupboard—he does *not* give : he might have lied about this, but lying is much more serious than churlishness. So he says that the door is fastened for the night, and the unbarring of an Eastern cottage door was more troublesome than the mere turning of a key. Besides, he is in bed, thoroughly settled for the night, with his family sleeping soundly near him, and to rouse them by getting up would be a pity, not to speak of the trouble of hushing the children asleep again. So, " I can't get up and give you anything," he says. Of course " can't " means " won't " ; he has unconsciously betrayed himself ; it is the " getting up " that is the real trouble—the disturbance of his comfort. He is considering his own position, not his friend's predicament, and he seeks to soothe his conscience by insinuating that a real friend would not be so unneighbourly as to disturb a whole household for three loaves. How much of this world's trouble goes unrelieved because we are too comfortable to be bothered !

The friend outside, however, becomes more insistent than ever : he is sure there is enough bread inside if he can only get at it, and that he is determined to do. It is more churlish to refuse a friend this small request than it is to make one cross by arousing him from sleep. So he persists in knocking and shouting, preventing the would-be sleeper from sleep and threatening to arouse the children after all with his noise ; till at last even this churl can stand it no longer, and for the sake of that very peace and comfort, which were his excuse for refusing, he rises and gives him all he needs—perhaps more than the three loaves asked. He was selfish in declining : he is selfish even in his giving, for it is less troublesome to get rid of his neighbour this way than to have him shouting and knocking outside for half an hour or more. It is here, as in the story of the widow and the Judge ; if you have confidence and persistence to worry one long enough you will gain your end at last, not from friendship or justice, but simply because they will not be bothered longer with you. Comfort, your enemy at first, is your friend and advocate in the end.

THE INTERPRETATION.—This Parable was spoken to encourage men in prayer, and teaches us to persist in the face of apparent denial.

(1) The centre of gravity is *outside* the house, not inside : we are to think chiefly of the one who prays, not of the manner of the answer. Both the story and experience suggest that there are times when God

Himself seems heedless and unresponsive, but it is only " seems," since we are taught the Certainty of an answer to our prayers : Jesus says that the true asker always succeeds (vv. 8-10). Yet the petitioner needs to be encouraged in his prayers ; it is man's approach to God that is before us—*the human side of prayer*. The picture to be retained is not that of the inside unresponsiveness, but that of the midnight darkness, the fact of an immediate need, the closed door and the persistent knocker and shouter without. That is how man shall pray : God will look after His own honour.

(2) *The one indispensable thing in Prayer is to keep on Praying.* " Pray, Pray, Pray ! " says Jesus. " Ask ! Seek ! Knock ! " Never lose heart, never give up hope ; take the kingdom of heaven by force. It is just as natural to ask God for His spiritual gifts, and to keep on asking, as it is natural (v. 5, " which of you ") for one to ask a friend for relief in an emergency, and to press for it. Prayer means desire ; Silence means indifference or hopelessness : and there are *no rewards for these*. Real desire is expressed in constant and earnest prayer ; delay shall only make the note of urgency stronger ; the longer the delay in reply, the more urgent the prayer ; delay should make for intensity, not cessation. Continuance is evidence of reality and deep desire ; there is such a thing as " wrestling in prayer " : " I will not let Thee go, except Thou bless me ! " Persistence in prayer is not only proof of intense desire, but it suggests a true appreciation of the blessing sought, capacity to receive it and character to use it. " God bestoweth His blessings there, where He

findeth the vessels *empty*." Pray!—until the answer comes.

(3) *For the Answer will come:* the Parable teaches us how to pray *successfully*. The only points of likeness between the cross friend in bed and God the Father, are that both possess the means of answering the cry of need, and that both do it: the motives of answering are not in question. Delay in the reply of God means the enhancement of His gifts and deeper joy on the receiver's side: it proves both God and man. Is not the most splendid encouragement to Prayer found in this Certainty of a Satisfying Answer? But—*when? That is behind the door;* Faith will pray and trust and hope and wait, sure that the door will open soon or late. Human friendship may fail (v. 8), yet earthly fatherhood does not play cruel tricks with children (vv. 11, 12), and still less will the Father in Heaven disappoint His children, when they pray (v. 13).

(4) In case some feel unsatisfied with the analogy of an earthly friend and neighbour whom one may bother into giving, and the distant Figure of a Father in Heaven, the story comes to us with the personal reassurance of the Lord Himself: " *I* say unto you, Knock, and it shall be opened unto you." If this incident from familiar experience contains no message to you of the Goodness and Graciousness of God, as Hearer and Giver, then believe *ME* when I tell you that God does always answer. Friendship is an encouragement to asking, fatherhood is even stronger, but the Fatherhood of God is beyond any question. " Prayer is a laying hold of God's highest willingness."

We need nothing more than this to bring us to our

knees in constant prayer when the spirit is sore and faint, or when the needs of the world lie heavy upon us. Only fools ask favours when ultimate repulse is certain : it is equal folly to refrain from prayer when an answer is sure ! Jesus is our guarantor of Prayer and its assured success.

THE SUBJECT OF PRAYER.—Having taught us how to pray, the Lord tells us something of what is to be the earnest object of our supplication. The chief figure in the Parable was definite ; he knew precisely what he needed—bread—food—" three loaves." Real, successful prayer must be definite, lest we ask amiss ; vagueness in prayer is folly and a beating of the air. In v. 13 the gift promised is " the Holy Spirit " : what S. Matthew, in the parallel verse (vii. 11), calls " good things." There is little difference, if any. The best thing man can ask from God is that which brings him nearest God—the very Spirit of God. Care for the material should not possess us when we come into God's presence ; He knoweth we have need of these things : it is the Bread of Life, the Food of the soul, that we shall make the determined object of our asking. All men have bodily hunger, but not all the hunger of the soul. Yet Power and Progress lie there. Labour or Charity will feed the body : God gives His Spirit to them that ask Him ; He is good to them that wait for Him.

If, in the lonely midnight of the soul, we ask as this man did, we shall not go away unsatisfied. How shall the Father deny to His children that very gift which makes them godly children ? You may ask your friend for bread : from God we shall ask what He alone can give—the gift of His Spirit. This is the Power which conquers temptation, purifies thought and imagination, reveals the higher and ever higher way of life, gives power over self and sin, and keeps us on the uplands of being. This is the equipment for service, for every gracious and effective ministry : does not the suggestion that by prayer we may *serve others,* lie in the fact that the asker of the story did so for the comfort of another ?

Which of us does not need much more of the Holy Spirit ? The questions is, *do we desire Him, and how deep is that desire ?*

> " I waited for the Lord my God,
>   and patiently did bear ;
> At length to me He did incline
>   my voice and cry to hear.
> He took me from a fearful pit,
>   and from the miry clay,
> And on a rock He set my feet,
>   establishing my way.
> He put a new song in my mouth,
>   our God to magnify :
> Many shall see it, and shall fear,
>   and on the Lord rely."
>
> Psalm 40, 1-3.

THE TWO DEBTORS

or,

FORGIVENESS AND GRATITUDE.

S. LUKE, vii. 36-50.

OCCASION.—This is a little bit of our Lord's Table-Talk. Only one constantly occupied with the deep things of God, and keenly observant of his fellows, could utter words so apt to the occasion and so true for all time. The little Parable shines and endures like a jewel. It explained the action of the unnamed woman, it reproved Simon and gave him a flash of self-revelation, and it vindicated His own conduct as "The Friend of Sinners." That honourable nickname has just been used by Jesus of Himself (v. 34), and S. Luke—who alone records this incident—fittingly sets it here as an example of its truth. It presents to us Jesus as the Friend of the street woman and also of the Pharisee : He is at home with all sorts, for He is The Friend of *Man*.

THE STORY.—We cannot separate the jewel from the setting, so the incident must be told at some length.

The Host of the occasion is a Pharisee named Simon. It says something for him that he had interest enough

117

in this new Teacher to make Him his guest : an unusual act for one of his class. He recognises the character of Jesus, and is so impressed by Him as to
wonder if He is a prophet—*i.e.*, one with special
commission from God. Wishing to learn more of
Him and to study Him at close quarters, he asks
Him to dinner. There is curiosity and patronage in
this rather than respect, not to speak of affection or
discipleship, for he does not extend to Him those
attentions which other guests of higher rank or closer
association receive.

The Woman. The presence of uninvited persons
in the guest-chamber was not unusual, sitting behind
those who reclined at table, and even joining in the
conversation. One comes on this occasion—the most
unlikely of all. That a woman of the town, known
to all for her evil life, should enter the house of a
Pharisee required no ordinary courage. She is either
absolutely shameless, or is influenced by some emotion
which drives all other considerations away. Notice
how the word " Pharisee " occurs four times in the
opening verses, with special point in vv. 37 and 39,
emphasising the unusual situation ; and notice
further how the word does *not* occur again, after the
lesson which Jesus teaches Simon !

What connection she may have had with the
Master we do not know : she may have been but one
of His many hearers, or there may have been some
unrecorded interview. The probability is the former,
since the narrative has no word suggesting a former
meeting. At all events she has been profoundly
moved by what she has heard from, and of, Jesus ;
it has changed her life ; she feels that she owes Him

her soul. How can she ever show her devotion and acknowledge her debt?

Her opportunity appears to have come when she hears that He is dining with Simon, and she determines to go there, to slip quietly behind Him, and anoint His feet as He reclines at table, with the rich perfumed oil carried in an alabastron suspended round her neck. But her feelings overcome her in the very moment of action: penitence, gratitude, devotion and nervous excitement at her surroundings, prove too much for her self-control, and she bursts into an uncontrollable flood of tears. Like a thunder-shower the drops rain down from the eyes in her bent head and fall upon His feet. Richer than any costly oil these unpremeditated tears are the very blood of her soul. She has no towel to wipe His feet, thus bedewed, so she stoops still further and loosens her hair—an immodest act for any Eastern woman, but she has gone too far to care for any criticism. Thus bending over the feet of Him she has come to honour, and screened by the mass of her loosened hair, she cannot refrain from pressing kisses upon them, time and again, with every surge of feeling, until composure at last returns, when she takes the perfumed oil and uses it upon them too. There was a time when her eyes, her lips, her hair and her perfume had another purpose: now they are her one means of honouring her Lord! The only human lips we read of as touching our Lord's body were those of this woman turning from ruin to Jesus, and those of Judas turning from Jesus to his ruin.

The Host again. How have these extraordinary proceedings been regarded by the host, Simon? (If he had noted nothing at first, the perfume of the oil would draw his attention.) It is to his credit that he does not think the worst. He has noted the woman, and is considering her in relationship to Jesus. He knows that Jesus is a good man, and yet here He allows this evil woman to touch Him! *That* no Pharisee would ever have permitted. Clearly, therefore, Jesus cannot know anything of her life. But if so, if He has no power of reading this woman's character, then He is but an ordinary person after all, and no special servant of God, no prophet. If Jesus does know, His standard of conduct must be very low to allow this : if He does not know, then He is no prophet of God. From Simon's point of view the dilemma is unanswerable.

But there is another point of view which he is soon to learn. Jesus is watching him and reads his judgments in his face, and proceeds to show in a few words that He not only knows what the woman is, but what Simon is, and thinks too. He proves Himself a prophet in a fashion the host never had dreamed of ! After politely claiming his attention Jesus tells a little story.

THE PARABLE.—Two men are in debt : one to the extent of 500 pence, the other, 50. Let us call it £15 and 30s. The sums are comparatively small ; so small that a well-to-do man like Simon would never suspect any personal application. Both debts are generously remitted by the creditor, and the question is then put : " Which of them, therefore, will love him most ? " The answer seems so easy and evident that Simon, with a touch of impatience and bewilderment at a story whose point or relevancy he cannot see, replies : " He, I suppose, to whom he forgave the most." With a touch of grave irony Jesus approves the answer, and having thus by the Socratic method involved Simon, He proceeds to show that he is self-convicted, at the same time defending the woman and Himself.

The Woman again. For the first time the Lord shows His consciousness of her presence and actions —to have done so sooner would only have increased her confusion—as He turns to her, and in emphatic and even passionate language contrasts her conduct with that of Simon, in his neglecting the immemorial grace of antiquity, the courtesies of a host, which she so far exceeds. There is dignified poetry in His words.

Simon had given Him no water.	She has given Him her tears, has made her hair a towel, a towel even for His feet.
Simon had given Him no kiss.	She has showered and pressed her kisses, her kisses even on His feet.
Simon had not graced Him with common oil; given no oil even for His head.	She has spent her perfumed ointment, on His feet.

Simon has asked Him to dinner : that is all. His interest in Jesus is very slight compared with this woman's. Surely her debt to Him must be very great, since she has shown such love : much love is ever the result of much forgiveness : has not Simon a moment ago acknowledged that ? This passionate demonstration of affection and devotion is the measure of her love, the result of sin forgiven, debt remitted.

This is her gratitude for the mercy she has found through Him. That her sins have been many Jesus fully allows; He knows her as well as, nay, better than, Simon. It is just because they have been so many that her action is so whole-hearted. Simon regarded her as an abandoned woman: Jesus sees her as abandoned to penitence and gratitude. He infers her many sins from her much love : the principle is applied backwards. Where there is little consciousness of sin, there is little sense of debt remitted, and so little expression of love. This last means Simon !

The end of the story is that she goes away with "saved" ringing in her ears and heart, while Simon falls to silence and self-examination : ever a better action than criticism. The Pharisee is now questioning himself. He had thought that Jesus did not know the woman : he has found that He knew her better than he did. It was just because He knew and understood her that He allowed her actions ; they came from a region which Simon had never thought possible for her, or any like her.

THE APPLICATION.—(1) On a narrow reading it would seem that v. 47 implied that it is only the great sinner who will show much love to Christ. It must be interpreted more widely than that. It is folly to think that we *must* sin much to love much. Because a man saved from drowning is profoundly grateful to his rescuer is no reason for you risking your life deliberately in the water. It is not reason or mercy, says Bunyan, for a man to abuse his Friend, to spit in Christ's face before kissing Him, to sin that grace may the more abound. " Felix culpa ! " is a dangerous motto. Yet he who *is* most conscious of the mercy of God, whatever his outward life may have been, is he who will show most devotion and sacrifice. He to whom God means most will praise most and best. The self-righteous, conscious of little obligation, are cold and perfunctory in their worship and gifts. *All are debtors* to God : but some are only 30s.-people ; others are in the £15 class. How do we rank ourselves ? Some, like Simon, seek to patronise Christ : others cannot do enough for him. They will give Him all, for He has given them their souls. They worship and adore. " Every deep human experience is a new vision of God." Simon got a new experience that day : surely he was grateful at last to Jesus for curing him of his blindness.

(2) There have been devotions, like this woman's, which shame the ordinary member of the Church : devotions of Life, like the missionaries of the early days of Missions ; of Art, as in the buildings and decorations of the churches of the Middle Ages ; of Wealth and Poetry and Service, of which there is no record but in Heaven. As with Simon, Prejudice, Pride and Prosperity prevent us from whole-hearted consecration, recking nothing of cost, or of what this and that one may think and say. There are many ways of anointing His feet : some grudge both the perfume and the tears. How much does Christ mean to you ? You cannot pay your debts to God, for all have sinned and come short of His glory ; but the gift of *yourself* is in your power, and no one can give more. Are you on your knees to Jesus ?

(3) There is another Lesson here : the delight our Lord had in all such uncalculating manifestations of

devotion, but this has been treated in those Parables which tell of the Joy in Finding one's Lost Possessions. Jesus loves to welcome the complete self-forgetting devotion of the heart. Those who, like this woman, have been whole-hearted in sin, become whole-hearted in service. They have cared nothing for opinion then, and care nothing now, but to please and honour Him. They had a great capacity of self-abandonment, and they have it still. Many of the greatest triumphs of the Gospel have been in degradation and corruption. What seems the extravagance of a revival meeting is often but the index to the greatness of His salvation.

Saul, who persecuted even to the death, becomes the Paul who counts all things but rubbish that he may win Christ, and who dies for his Lord. And Saul was a Pharisee! So even this Pharisee, Simon, found that day how he owed his soul and new understanding of God and man to Jesus. His silence reveals his feelings, as the woman's tears revealed her heart.

THE UNFORGIVING SERVANT

or,

THE SIN THAT LOSES THE KINGDOM.

S. MATTHEW, xviii. 21-35.

NOBODY acts perfectly to everybody, perhaps not to anybody; and some behave very badly to others in their power. When an offender seems really penitent and sorry, and you forgive the fault, and yet experience from him the same wrong again, what are you to do? At what point in such repeated wrong are you to forget mercy and proceed to punishment? Jesus here tells us how a good citizen of the Kingdom of God will act.

THE QUESTION.—There has been talk about Offences, and Peter has become anxious over the matter of Forgiveness, so when an opportunity came he questions the Master as to how often one should forgive: could it be as often as seven times? That must surely be the maximum. It went further than the Rabbis went, so to some extent Peter is profiting by Jesus' company and teaching.

But the reply is bewildering to him, and perhaps to us. Not seven times, says Jesus: seventy times seven is more like it; acts of Forgiveness are not to be counted. Those who live in a Kingdom of Grace must show nothing but Grace : it is the only language of God's children. God has given, and forgiven, us so much ; how can we deny our brother a trifle ? God's attitude to man is mercy : what is your attitude to your brother ? It is only by His forgiveness that you enter His Presence and enjoy His Favour, and His servants must show His Spirit. Unless you have learned God's language you cannot understand Him, or enter His doors. Unless you reflect the sunshine, you must live in the darkness. Tenderness is the other side of Gratitude : those who show no mercy neither understand it nor experience it. So to bring home to His hearers the Relationship of God to man, and man to his fellows, Jesus tells this simple story of a king and his servants. It needs no re-telling, only careful and prayerful re-reading.

An Eastern Story.—There is one feature in the story, however, which must not be passed over : its strongly marked Eastern character. This appears in several points foreign to us of the West.

There is the rapid change of fortune where we see a man of position deprived of everything but life in a moment, and just as rapidly having the whole restored to him again. There is the unquestioned power of the monarch at whose word this takes place, and the confidence that such an experience will make an offender very chary of incurring blame again. There is the carelessness in finance which could allow such peculations to take place over a long period, and the selfishness which takes advantage of such opportunities. There is the law that a man's wife and family are regarded as his property, capable of being sold to repay debts. And there is the extraordinary mixture of rank and class which induces one to grasp at a debt of a few pounds while he is in a position to amass millions.

LESSON.—The interpretative verse is the last one : " So likewise shall my heavenly Father do also unto you, if ye from the heart forgive not every one his brother their trespasses." The word " Father " is strongly introduced here, for the Parable is indeed " the Parable of the outraged Love of God." He who betakes himself to his knees before Heaven must recall *that*, when a fellow creature is on his knees before him : the street is to be a reflection of the Church, and the home and office a repetition of the closet. To savour the Divine Mercy at the Holy Table one day, and to break another's heart by our implacability next day, shows that the former has not been appreciated. It is to crucify the Lord afresh and put Him to an open shame. To live under grace and act under justice is impossible. A forgiving God does not forgive an unforgiving spirit. " As certainly as there is no Kingdom of God without the forgiveness which we receive, so certainly there is no Kingdom of God without the forgiveness which we bestow." The *power* of forgiveness implies the *duty*.

A chance meeting with his fellow-servant (perhaps going to an examination similar to his own) as the restored offender left the audience chamber, proved the unreality of his penitence, the superficiality of his confession. It is the casual and ordinary things which test the sincerity of our spiritual experiences.

Conduct to men tests our converse with God. The little things of fretting day test our eternal standing in Heaven. "If this man's heart had been charged with mercy, it would have discharged." "The surest test by which to distinguish between true penitence and spasmodic emotion is to set about the common duties of life. If, amid the distractions of these things, he loses his contrition, it is evident that he never was earnestly contrite; that his was mere excited sensibility and not inward feeling." At all times shall men prove themselves children of the Father to Whom they pray: "Forgive us our debts as we forgive our debtors."

This concluding verse does not say that our Forgiveness is the cause of the Divine Mercy, but that it is a *Condition*. Unless we are able to forgive we are unable to accept Forgiveness. The door of God's mercy is opened from the inside, but it opens only to those who approach it by the road of human mercy. A merciless man shuts the door, but cannot open it: shuts it on himself. You cannot understand a language you have never learned. Arnot uses the rather pertinent simile of two cog-wheels, the larger driving the less. When the less is out of gear or position it does not receive the right impulse from the other and it becomes idle and ineffective. "Keep yourselves *in* the love of God."

THE ANSWER.—Is there ever a time when we are justified in refusing Forgiveness to an offending and penitent fellow-servant? [Remember that the Parable deals only with faults between one individual and another: the determining word is "brother"

(vv. 21, 35)]. Take the matter into the Divine Presence and look at it there : let the shadow of the Cross fall upon the problem. Let the Mercy of God be ever the determining factor in your conduct to others : that is the summary of Jesus' Lesson. Remember also that *Forgiveness means Power*, not Weakness. It is only strength that can forgive : one must be in your power ere you can forgive him. He must feel and acknowledge that he owes you something which he cannot pay in other payment than penitence and the crave for forgiveness. A weak man may enjoy the sense of power to torture and abuse the offender : a strong man will cancel the debt and see the sunshine in his brother's face, the reflection of the Divine Mercy in his own heart. Portia has summed it up :—

> " It is an attribute of God Himself ;
> And earthly power doth then show likest God's
> When mercy seasons justice. Therefore, Jew,
> Though justice be thy plea, consider this,
> That, in the course of justice, none of us
> Should see salvation : we do pray for mercy ;
> And that same prayer doth teach us all to render
> The deeds of mercy."

After all, shall we be appreciably poorer if we forgive : shall we not be very appreciably stronger, happier and better, if we rise to it ? A selfish satisfaction of temporary power cannot be weighed against that which " blesseth him that gives, and him that takes." Our mutual debts are trifling things, but may yet prove very costly, for they may make us lose the peace of God. When self poisons the soul, it begins to die. " When one thinks of all one might have done, and all one ought to have done, there seems to be no time left to think of wrongs we have received or benefits we have missed " (Benj. Jowett).

All of us, if we have any decency at all, condemn the harshness of the unforgiving servant, just as his fellows at court condemned him : the trouble arises in failing to recognise the parallel situation in our own experience. *What do we each owe to God ?* The perfect service of an obedient life. And what have we to offer Him ? A shrine unswept, an altar whose fires are almost dead, sacrifices few and poor. Yet He covers our sins as with a cloud, and He abundantly pardons. He removes our iniquities far from us ; He gives rest to the heavy-laden and opens His heart to the returning Prodigal. The broken and contrite heart He does not despise. To one who knows these things, all the frets of our fellows are but trifles. " God comforts us, not to make us comfortable, but to make us comforters."

WISE AND STUPID HOUSE-BUILDING

or,

ACTION IS THE SURE FOUNDATION.

S. MATTHEW, vii. 21-27.   S. LUKE, vi. 46-49.

THIS Parable has special importance from its *position* at the close of the Sermon ; it contains a final warning and promise. Very simply also the Speaker says that in our attitude towards His Words lies our spiritual peace and permanence or our spiritual ruin. " It is the consciousness that the Speaker is nothing less than the final Judge of all which makes this Parable, with which the sermon closes, the most solemn and overpowering of all the words of Jesus " (Denney).

A " House " is a beautifully chosen emblem for one's Religion—one's constant dwelling-place ; but the tempting allegorising of the details of the story is to be shunned.

(1) FOUNDATIONS.—The essential—in a very literal way, the fundamental—difference between the two builders is, that one did not build until he had made sure of a foundation, while the other disregarded that initial precaution. Perhaps he was in a hurry,

perhaps he was simply stupid. S. Luke's account emphasises this difference—"digged, went deep, upon the rock"; the other—"without a foundation." It is not a question of *what* they built : the houses may have been exactly the same, or the stupid man's may have seemed even the finer ; nor is it a question of *on* what they built : in Palestine rock was best, in some countries sand is safer ; but the question goes back to a first principle—*how* did they build, did they consider their foundations at all, did they reckon with the possibility of storm and so seek to ensure permanence and stability ? It is foul weather that tests foundations.

In ordinary experience, of course, only a stupid man would neglect this all-important question, and our Lord says he *is* a "stupid" who acts so ; but this only makes the charge more stinging that in Religion such action is no uncommon thing, that there are more fools in religion than know themselves such. House-building and Christian Character are serious things, to be gone about with consideration, forethought and determination. It is just as natural for man to have a Religion as to have a House, but let him apply common and serious sense to both !

(2) CONDUCT.—What is the equivalent of making sure of a foundation in the building of a Christian Life and Character ? Jesus says it is *Action :* "he that doeth My words." We must have more than Christian principles, admirations, enthusiasms and creeds, saying, "Lord, Lord" ; we must adjust our conduct to these principles. Definite, personal obedience to all He says is essential to spiritual

permanence. " A life in which conduct does not fairly well accord with principles is a silly life ; and that conduct can only be made to accord with principles by means of daily examination, reflection and resolution " (Bennett).

To be a follower of Jesus means the exercise of effort, the taking of trouble. At the last the difference will be evident between the Superficial Religion of Words and Sentiment and the Fundamental Religion of Will and Action. Obedience is Strength. Young people in church and school must seek at once to *do* what they *know* Jesus commands them ; that way alone lies security, hope and strength to resist allurement and temptation. There is no security without conduct ; a Christian life and character rest upon action. An unfounded, unsafe life is one which has Profession without Performance, and when stress and strain and foul weather come storming upon it there is catastrophe !

(3) WILL.—But Christian Obedience is not visible Action alone ; it includes the Inner Life with such virtues and graces as are given in the Beatitudes and throughout the Sermon. We must dig deep, down through care, selfishness, sloth, vanity, greed, revenge, passion and littleness, down to the bedrock of the Will, and make it His. We must determine to conquer within, to master all appetites, passions and inclinations which are hostile to the spirit of Christ, and to bring every thought into His obedience. Christian Action follows from Christian Being. Religion must go deep and grip the whole man. Searchingly and sincerely to seek to put the Sermon on the Mount

into action will prove the safe foundation for discipleship.

Without determined realising of Christ's will for yourself, your Christian Profession is no better than foolishness, and the day will declare it! The strong man is he who *acts* and *is*. The man who stays is the man who stays with God. To abide in Him is to stand fast for ever. This *do*, and ye shall live.

V.

EPILOGUE:
THE CHRISTIAN SCRIBE.

THE CHRISTIAN SCRIBE

or,

THE SECRET OF THE PREACHER'S FRESHNESS.

S. MATTHEW, xiii. 52.

ONE should begin by reading this verse either in the Revised Version or in Moffatt's translation.

It is an example of its own teaching, for it links the old and the new : when the " scribe " of the Old Dispensation becomes " the disciple of the kingdom," he has a storehouse rich in variety, from Moses till his own day. This is the Charter of Freedom in the presentation of eternal truth.

EXPOSITION.—(1) *The scribes* of our Lord's day formed a learned order of the Pharisees, who devoted time and talent to the study and application of the Mosiac Law. No detail escaped them ; they revelled in them. They were known as " The Counters," since they had actually counted the letters in it, finding the central letter in Lev., xi. 42. The " letter " to them mattered more than the " spirit " ; and the result was distinctly deadening.

When such a scribe has become a disciple of The Kingdom with its new approach to God and a new devotion to His Will and Law, the same assiduity and thoroughness will enrich his output in an extraordinary fashion. There will be new life and power, new and attractive substance. To sit at the feet of Jesus and catch His spirit will prevent any teacher of religious truth from ever becoming stale and dull. The stagnant pool becomes a sparkling spring. He is like the unchanging change of Nature, each new season bringing new stores of grain. His words reach his own age, because he has the secret of the ages.

(2) *The Master* Himself is the perfect example of what He teaches here. He did not come to destroy the Law : He came to fulfil it, but, as He taught, the hearers felt that there was something new and different, for " He taught with authority, and not as the scribes." He is perfectly familiar with the past : " ye have heard," He says more than once ; and then comes the startling novelty, " but I say unto you."

His illustrations were familiar and old—old as Nature, old as husbandry and fishing, old as cooking and trading, old as wine-making and travel, old as selfish sons and friendly feasts, old as the red of sunset and the welcome rain. But they rang with a fresh tone and spoke of Divine and human things in a manner which both delighted and surprised. He showed men what the Sabbath was ; not a grave in which to bury one's humanity, but a road beneath men's feet by which they went to God and to the hearts of their fellows. He showed men the purity which God wished, not of cup and platter, but of motive and desire. He showed men what God's attitude to mankind was ; like the rain and sun which take no heed of nationality or desert. He made the fireside speak of " The Father " ; He found lessons of mercy in the courts of kings.

He was no John with the axe and winnowing fan of punishment : rather did He earn the title, " The Friend of Publicans and Sinners," and taught that all men should be friends of such, if they wished to share in Heaven's music. He laid no burden upon religious life and practice, except that " yoke " of His which is so easy and so light. His school has the secret of rest to weary souls.

APPLICATION.—*The Christian Teacher* of every age must hold Christ by one hand, while with the other he ranges the world and lays its treasures at his Master's feet. All that Science and Art can give are his to use : every truth of criticism and scholarship becomes his servant : the Creeds are but milestones on the road of Christian thought, not its goal and end—the Shorter Catechism says neither " Love " nor " Father " when it tries to tell us about God—there is advance and gain in every century in the understanding and expression of Divine Truth. The heavens declare the glory of God and the firmament shows forth His handiwork to men of our day, in a fashion poles distant from the understanding of Abraham, Moses, David, or Isaiah. The telescope has pierced the depths and weighed the stars, and studded with new glittering gems the throne of the Almighty.

As " bird and flower made plain of old the Lesson of the Teacher," so the pulpit and platform of to-day have treasures both old and new for the enrichment and sustenance of men. The arrows of truth must be ground sharp upon the whirling stones of one's own day, but the metal of the barb and the feather which guides are found in Nature's stores, eternal as life among the hills.

Everything that is novel is not true, but every truth was once " news," and truths from every quarter of human study shall only enrich the true disciple of the Kingdom, for the Kingdom of Truth has but one King, though its citizens may be labouring continents apart. He has yet many things to say unto us, and He has promised His Spirit to guide us into all the truth. Revelation did not close with the closing of the Canon, and God has still many pages for men to turn. Let us read them upon our knees !

Printed in Great Britain by
WILLIAM BLACKWOOD & SONS LTD.